BOYS OF
THE
BURNING SKY

Marine Corsair Pilots of
Operation Iceberg

VMF-322 and the Close Air
Support on Okinawa

Frederick Martine Rauschenbach
Jr.

Martine Publishing

ISBN-13: 9798995269915
ISBN-10: 1477123456

Cover design by: Natalie Rauschenbach
Library of Congress Control Number: 2018675309
Printed in the United States of America

"Don't Pull Up Until the Green Turns to Grass."

FREDERICK M. RAUSCHENBACH, MAJOR, C.O. VMF-322,
OKINAWA 1945

CHAPTER 1 – LAMINAR FLOW...1

CHAPTER 2 – DIFFERENT ROADS...8

CHAPTER 3 – N.A.S. PENSACOLA.. 17

CHAPTER 4 – THE GATES OF HELL.. 22

CHAPTER 5 – SUMMER KILLS 31

CHAPTER 6 – SOLO 37

CHAPTER 7 – GOLD WINGS 43

CHAPTER 8 – BUTTERBARS 45

CHAPTER 9 – HOLDOVERS 47

CHAPTER 10 – THE DISRUPTOR 49

CHAPTER 11 – DOWN TIME 52

CHAPTER 12 – FLY LIKE AN EAGLE 54

CHAPTER 13 – WING AND A PRAYER 57

CHAPTER 14 – RESIGNATION 60

CHAPTER 15 – SILENT ARRIVAL... 63

CHAPTER 16 – WINGS OF ANGELS.. 65

CHAPTER 17 – WEDDING BELLS 68

CHAPTER 18 – ANCHOR POINTS 70

CHAPTER 19 – PROJECT GEORGE 72

CHAPTER 20 – INFAMY.. 79

CHAPTER 21 – GLIDER GROUP 71.. 81

CHAPTER 22 – A PATH NOT TAKEN.. 84

CHAPTER 23 – LOUD ARRIVAL... 86

CHAPTER 24 – VMF-321 (OJT)... 92

CHAPTER 25 – COMMAND.. 94

CHAPTER 26 – "YOU COMMAND, I CONTROL" 99

CHAPTER 27 – MOVEMENT WEST 109

CHAPTER 28 – HAWAI'I... 116

CHAPTER 29 – MCAS EWA 119

CHAPTER 30 – C.W. "SKID" RAUSCHENBACH 126

CHAPTER 31 – ESPIRITU SANTO 133

CHAPTER 32 – ELAINE 138

CHAPTER 33 – SECRET DESTINATION 148

CHAPTER 34 – OPERATION ICEBERG 151

CHAPTER 35 – GROUNDED 160

CHAPTER 36 — ANGELS OF OKINAWA 164

CHAPTER 37 — FIRST BLOOD 173

CHAPTER 38 – CLOSE AIR SUPPORT (CAS) 188

CHAPTER 39 – KAKAZU 197

CHAPTER 40 – MEATGRINDER 208

CHAPTER 41 – MAY 1945 222

CHAPTER 42 – THE 3RD ECHELON 224

CHAPTER 43 – SHURI LINE 229

CHAPTER 44 – ACCIDENTS WAITING TO HAPPEN 234

CHAPTER 45 – THE NICK ENGAGEMENT 239

CHAPTER 46 – CHOCOLATE DROP HILL 242

CHAPTER 47 – THE LAST RETURN 250

CHAPTER 48 – WANA RIDGE /WANA DRAW 259

CHAPTER 49 – FAREWELL 267

EPILOGUE 270

AUTHOR'S HISTORICAL NOTE 277

PHOTO CREDITS 280

DEDICATION 281

ACKNOWLEDGEMENTS 282

INTRODUCTION

I didn't know my father well as a child. I grew up in a middle-class neighborhood of Southern California, in a house with five older sisters and my single mother. My father lived across town. I only saw him on birthdays and holidays, although I do remember a summer camping trip and fishing trip off Santa Monica. He and Mom didn't exactly socialize.

As a 6- or 7-year-old child, I remember sitting cross-legged for hours, with this monster of a red leather-bound book.

I wasn't fascinated by war, but I certainly was captivated by the images. The crime of war, the glory of war, the sacrifices of individuals and nations, the notion of self-less service. WW II was still very fresh socially, and service would come up in conversations that I would eavesdrop on at mother's parties, or patriotic events in the community. I knew my father had served in the Marines, as a pilot, and had fought in the Pacific.

Mom eventually remarried and we moved away but remained in Southern California. Visits to or from Dad became less frequent.

At 17, I walked into an Army recruiting office. In 1975, I visited my father before departing for Boot

Camp at Ft. Polk, LA. There wasn't much to say between us. Conversations always
	seemed an inconvenience, or a consequence forced upon him from a previous choice. But he pulled down off the wall his USMC saber, wished me luck, and gave it to me.

	Off I went to slay dragons.
	#

	Fast-forward to the 21st Century. After a military career, a family, a civilian career, I find myself a grandfather. I realized one day that I am the last male in my family line. I felt incumbent somehow, to not let my father's story go untold.

	So, I started to dig. To document, research, verify and validate his military experiences.

	He had dropped out of college to join the Marine Corps and eventually walked away from it with a Master of Science in Aeronautical Engineering from the Massachusetts Institute of Technology (M.I.T.) to pursue a civilian career in the space industry. He resigned his commission in 1955 as an LTC(P), with less than 15 years in and at the ripe old age of 35.

	However, as I was researching him, I kept running across these same individuals serving with or around my father: **Jack Robinson Mathis, Charleton Bidwell Ivey Sr., George Axtell Jr., Gregory Boyington, Edmund Fryer Overend, Hugh Irving Russell, Douglas Beebe Lenardson, Richard Maurice Day**, and **Quinton Roy Johns**.

	I realized, these were *all* extraordinary men, and they were an exceptional group, whose paths were connected by war.

	That connection to each other, to the skies they flew in, and the war they fought in was amplified and solidified by the warbird F4U-Corsairs and other aircraft they mastered.

They were young. All so young. A handful of names among the many that should not be forgotten. You could write a book about each of them.

So yes, this is a tribute to my father. But it also attempts to unveil the untold exceptional relationships between these **"BOYS OF THE BURNING SKY"**—their skill, courage, leadership, and sacrifices.

While the events are based on historical data, this is still a work of fiction when it comes to the men, relationships, and the Corps. I am not a historian. I am not an aviator. I am not a Marine. So, I hope you will allow for whatever omissions, inaccuracies, imagination that I may have filtered into my telling of this story. It is very much a true story. If I could ask my father today to shed some light on his personal thoughts, relationships, conversations, and events, it would probably be a better story.

Frederick Martine Rauschenbach Jr.

PREFACE

This coming-of-age story is about young warriors, fighter pilots, living on the edge of aviation, fire support, technology and survival. Brothers-In-Arms. This story is also about Close Air Support (CAS), which is air action by fixed or rotary-winged aircraft against hostile targets in close proximity to friendly forces.

CAS requires detailed, real-time integration with the fire and movement of ground forces to destroy or neutralize enemy positions.

CAS is essential for breaking enemy lines or providing immediate fire support, often requiring close coordination to prevent friendly fire.

Unlike Air Interdiction, which targets enemy assets further from the front lines (in air, on water, and to the rear) to prevent them from reaching the battle, CAS directly supports troops already engaged in combat with the enemy.

The CAS mission is a different beast than air-to-air or bomber escort missions. It is a different kind of up close and personal.

Ask the fellow with his face in the mud.

CHAPTER 1 – LAMINAR FLOW

New York City, Spring 1939

Frederick Rauschenbach, 19, sat near the back of a classroom that was already too warm. Spring light slanted through the open windows of City College, catching dust in its path and holding it there suspended as if the air itself had decided to pause. The radiators still clicked faintly beneath the windows despite the season, metal expanding and contracting out of habit rather than necessity. Outside, along Convent Avenue, the first green buds had begun to assert themselves on the bare branches—small, stubborn signs of movement that did not ask permission.

Frederick half-listened to the professor with his notebook open and his pencil moving steadily. His handwriting was precise, almost architectural. Equations filled the page—arrows, symbols, vectors marching in disciplined rows. Diagrams of airflow curved neatly around wing sections drawn to scale. Laminar flow: predictable, ordered, and obedient, so long as it was treated properly.

Air behaved, he had learned, when men respected its rules.

Professor Mallory spoke without urgency. His voice carried the confidence of someone whose subject matter obeyed him, folding into the scrape of chalk and the low hum of the building itself. He spoke of boundary layers and coefficients, of how turbulence could be postponed, not eliminated. The lecture was familiar. Fred had heard it before and understood it.

That was his problem. He knew he was wasting time, and time was of the essence.

Fred's eyes drifted briefly to the window. Somewhere beyond the classroom, beyond the city, aircraft were already crossing oceans that pretended to be empty. Newspapers had been full of it—Germany absorbing countries the way a tide absorbs sand, Japan pushing outward across the Pacific with deliberate intentions. The world was moving, compressing. The equations on the page did not account for human urgency.

He eased open his chemistry textbook just enough to reveal the folded newspaper tucked inside it. He hadn't brought it for the headlines. He already knew how they read. What stopped him was a small block of print, direct and unadorned, bordered by white space that made it feel deliberate.

MARINE CORPS RECRUITING
SCOUT BOMBING SQUADRON
WANTED:
AVIATION MECHANICS
AND
FLIGHT CADETS
Apply today 2:00 P.M. at Floyd Bennett Field

He read it once. Then again.

There was no thrill. No rush of blood or cinematic certainty. What settled instead was recognition—quiet, complete. Something already decided, simply waiting for him to acknowledge it. Outside, branches stirred in the mild breeze. Inside his chest, something shifted with them, aligning.

Professor Mallory turned back to the board, chalk tapping twice for emphasis. Fred folded the paper carefully along its crease and slid it into the inside pocket of his jacket. His notebook remained open on the desk, equations unfinished, airflow unresolved.

Fred stood. The chair legs scraped against the floor, louder than necessary, a brief protest. No one noticed. Or if they did, they chose not to. College classrooms were full of men practicing disappearance. He gathered his coat and stepped into the aisle. For a moment—only a moment—he half-expected a voice to stop him. A question. A reminder. A hand on his sleeve pointing him back toward certainty. Nothing came.

The hallway smelled of wax, old paper, and damp wool coats. His footsteps echoed on the stairs, each one sounding heavier than the last, not with regret but with consequence.

By the time he reached the sunlight outside, the decision had finished settling, locking into place like a control surface trimmed for flight.

Engineering depended on certainty. The Marine Corps required motion.

Fred stepped onto the street and did not look back. Above him, the sky was clear and indifferent, a pale blue stretched wide enough for anyone willing to enter it, yet unforgiving to those who hesitated. Somewhere south, runways were already waiting.

\#

Fred packed carefully. Not because there was much to bring—only what fit into a canvas duffel— but because care was the last form of order available to him. Shirts folded flat. Socks rolled tight. One spare pair of shoes placed heel-to-toe along the bottom. His notebook slid in last; the pencil tucked inside its spine. Each movement was deliberate, measured, as if precision itself might stave off doubt. He had enlisted in the Marine Corps Reserve, as an airplane mechanic, and had spent the last several months waiting for an Aviation Cadet slot to open. His application had been approved, and his orders had arrived.

The apartment above the bodega held its familiar smells: coffee grounds, varnished wood, the faint trace of tobacco smoke that clung to the curtains no matter how often they were aired out. A place built on routine. On staying. The walls had absorbed years of repetition—meals eaten, news read, arguments deferred.

His father stood near the doorway, arms folded, watching without comment. He had paced earlier, the way men do when they cannot intervene but refuse to leave. Now he was still—a man restraining words he already knew wouldn't land. "This isn't the plan," he said at last.

Fred pressed the final shirt smooth, then tightened the strap on the duffel. "I know."

"You were doing well. Engineering is solid. Predictable. It keeps a man where he belongs." He sighed and stared at the window above the sink.

Fred lifted the duffel slightly, testing the weight, feeling its pull against his shoulder.

He lifted a framed photo from the mantel of a man, older than him, in Navy uniform. "So do submarines," Fred said.

His father's eyes shifted from the skyline to his son's unsmiling face "Skid chose that life," he said carefully. "Your brother chose that life."

"He chose to move," Fred replied. Silence settled between them.

Charlie Rauschenbach, or "Skid," wasn't spoken of often in the house. Not because of distance, but because of depth. Older by more than a decade. Born of a different chapter. A half-brother who had already slipped beneath the surface of the world, volunteering for a kind of war that offered no burning sky at all.

"He's a torpedoman," Fred said. "On boats that won't surface if things go wrong."

"That's different."

"It's not. It's just underwater."

His father turned away then, adjusting the photo Fred had set back down fondly. Skid squinting against the sun on a pier somewhere Fred had never seen. A man who trusted steel pressure hulls and darkness the way others trusted air. From the kitchen doorway, Fred's mother Marie, watched quietly, hands folded against her apron.

"You'll write," she said.

"Yes."

"You'll eat."

He nodded.

His mother was Jewish and had fled Russia in 1914. This war in Europe haunted her. After WW I, she never was able to contact the family she left behind.

His uncle John entered without knocking, his coat remaining on. He had always moved that way, as if departures required readiness rather than ceremony. He crossed the room and placed a small velvet pouch into Fred's open hand. "For the sky," he said.

Fred loosened the drawstring. Inside lay a silver medallion, worn smooth with age and touch. St. Joseph of Cupertino.

"Patron saint of pilots," his uncle said. "And the impossible."

Fred turned it over between his fingers. The edge was rubbed thin. Not ornamental. Used.

"He was an Italian monk," his uncle continued. "Couldn't read Latin properly. Barely passed his exams. But he prayed and fasted and somehow—somehow—kept lifting off the ground. Said faith made him lighter. I wore it when I performed. My trapeze work. No net some nights. It wasn't luck. It was a reminder not to rush the moment before lift. To respect gravity—and let go of it anyway."

Fred closed his fingers around the metal. It was cool. Dense.

"Skid trusts steel and pressure," his uncle said. "You'll trust air. Either way, something holds. Or it doesn't."

The street outside was louder than the apartment had been. They all stepped down from the stoop, the duffel strap cut firm across Fred's shoulder as he let the door close behind them. The weight of it lingered—not the bag, but the fact that he might never return. The bodega's metal gate was halfway down for the evening, rattling as a delivery truck idled at the curb. The smell of bread and gasoline mixed in the cooling air. Fred did not look back.

The walk to the subway was familiar enough that his feet carried him without thought, past storefronts closing early, past faces that registered him only as another man moving with purpose. The city had no patience for hesitation and no memory for goodbyes.

At Central Station, the ceiling vanished upward into shadow. Steam drifted across the platforms. Porters threaded through the crowds with practiced indifference. Every sound echoed—footsteps, whistles, voices layered over one another. Time folded in on itself. Steam hissed. Shoes scuffed on concrete. Voices echoed with departure. Fred hugged his mother once—tight, quickly stepping back before the moment demanded more.

His father placed a firm hand on his shoulder. "Be careful," he said. Care, he would find out, was already a new currency.

The coach car smelled of coats, iron, and yesterday's paper. A man sat near the door, cap tilted back, talking quietly to no one.

Fred noticed the man's hands—scarred, confident—and wondered, briefly, how far below the surface his brother was that night.

As the train pulled away, New York slid backward through the glass. Brick. Steel. Noise. Distance grew without argument. Fred touched the chain once around his neck, feeling the weight of St. Joseph against his palm.

Somewhere ahead were airfields and men he had not yet met, men whose names would one day matter more than equations ever had. A sky that did not tolerate mistakes. A burning sky already changing shape beyond the horizon. Fred leaned back against the seat, eyes forward. The decision was no longer behind him. It was moving him.

Figure 1. Fred Rauschenbach, age 19.

CHAPTER 2 – DIFFERENT ROADS

His train rolled south through the night, pulling Fred away from the city mile by mile.

Central Station collapsed behind him into steel and shadow, its vaulted ceiling swallowed by darkness as the train gathered speed. The rhythm of the rails replaced the city's noise—steady, mechanical, unarguable. Fred slept in fragments. Twenty minutes. Forty. An hour if he was lucky. He woke to stations without names, to the hiss of air brakes, to the muffled calls of conductors passing down the aisle with practiced indifference. Each time he opened his eyes, the world outside had shifted. By morning, New York had already begun to feel theoretical.

The car smelled of bad breath, stale coffee, and metal heated by friction. Men adjusted coats, folded newspapers, rubbed sleep from their faces. Fred watched unfamiliar towns pass the window—grain silos, water towers, clapboard stations—places built to be transited, not remembered. The farther south they traveled, the flatter the land became. The sky widened. Heat pressed through the glass with a damp insistence that felt southern even before it was.

He did not read. He did not write. He let motion do its work.

At a stop in Virginia, a radio on the platform crackled through a report about Prague. No one commented. A man folded his paper carefully and slid it into his pocket as if news itself were fragile. The train moved on.

Across the country, other men were moving too, each of them unaware of the other. In Massachusetts, **George Axtell** stood on a narrow platform with his leather suitcase placed squarely at his feet. His father faced him without ceremony, hat off despite the cold, posture straight in a way that suggested decades of correction. They shook hands. The grip lingered—firm, measuring—neither man willing to release first. Words were unnecessary. Expectations had already been set.

When Axtell boarded the bus, he chose the window seat and sat upright, hands folded on the suitcase handle. Familiar streets slid away. He cataloged them unconsciously: the mill, the church, the corner where boys learned to smoke. He did not turn around. He believed in momentum.

In Michigan, **Douglas Lenardson** waited beside a civilian mail plane with his gear stacked neatly at his feet. He checked his manuals once, then again, fingers tracing the margins as if they might escape. The pilot eyed him briefly, young, careful, too serious. Lenardson did not speak. When the propeller spun up and the aircraft lifted, his shoulders dropped for the first time in months. He smiled—not with joy, but relief.

Illinois spurred **Jack Mathis** away in the back of a delivery truck, duffel lashed down with twine. Field dust hung in the air, coating his hair, his jacket, his teeth. He didn't brush it off. It felt like proof. The road unfurled behind him in long, easy lines. He leaned against the side panel, grinning into the wind, already convinced he would master whatever came next. Confidence came easily to him. Consequence had not yet arrived.

Wisconsin saw **Hugh Russell** tip his hat to a girl on the platform and board a train without looking back. The engine lurched forward. He remained standing, balanced easily as the car began to move. Only after the countryside started to slide past did he take a seat. He had learned early that balance mattered most once motion was unavoidable.

From Oregon, **Edmund Overend** climbed into a Navy recruiter's car at dawn, a cigarette already lit. He crushed it beneath his heel without ceremony and folded his orders into his coat pocket. The recruiter talked.

Overend did not listen. This was not the beginning. It was a return—to structure, to hierarchy, to something that did not require explanation.

Charlton Ivey boarded a Greyhound bus in South Carolina, with a stack of flight manuals pressed tight to his chest. He sat forward, eyes ahead, mind arranging checklists. He had already calculated what he could control and dismissed the rest. Fear, to him, was an accounting problem.

Almost missing his train, **Quinton Johns** sprinted down the Georgia platform laughing, leaping for the handrail as the caboose began to roll. He waved at siblings who grew smaller with each second, grin fixed in place, as if charm alone might bend uncertainty. Even as the train gained speed, he leaned out just long enough to make them laugh again.

The men did not know they were destined to work on the same team, or that their service together would have a cost.

\#

Fred watched the land open beyond his window. The density of the city gave way to space. The air smelled of pine and damp soil. At a stop outside Raleigh, a sailor boarded and sat across from him. Torpedoman's insignia stitched cleanly onto his sleeve. Fred nodded. The sailor nodded back. That was enough. The train pressed on. Afternoon bled into evening. The car grew quieter. Men dozed. Others stared ahead, already separating from who they had been.

When Pensacola finally appeared, it was night. Floodlights carved the base gate out of darkness. Buses idled in uneven rows, engines rumbling low. Young men stepped down and were immediately gathered, ordered, aligned. Names were called. Papers checked. Voices

sharpened. The air was thick with salt and fuel and
something metallic beneath it all.

Fred set his duffel down at his feet. Nearby, a man
with wire-rimmed glasses adjusted his pack strap twice
before committing. Another rolled his shoulders like a
fighter warming up. Someone laughed too loudly.
Someone else stared straight ahead, unmoving. Under the
lights, faces flattened. Individuality evaporated. Beyond
the gate waited barracks, classrooms, runways: systems
were already alive. Above them hung a sky that would
soon decide who stayed and who vanished.

They were herded into temporary barracks and
able to get some shut eye. Processing would start early.

The next morning, they were fed and marched over
to In-Processing. Fred sat still, St. Joseph medallion warm
against his chest, listening as names were called. When he
heard his name, he answered clearly and stepped forward.

The clerk's pen scratched across the form, slower
now. "City College," he repeated, as if testing it.
"Engineering?"

"Yes."

The clerk made a small sound—neither approval
nor dismissal—and stamped the page. The ink bled
slightly, imperfect. Fred watched it spread. "You'll get
medical next," the clerk said. "Then gear issue. Then
barracks. Don't wander. You wander; you get noticed."
Fred took the packet, stepped aside and took a seat.

The room was already filling with men clutching
identical folders, shuffling forward in uneven lines. The
Corps did not rush them. It lets them wait. Waiting, Fred
realized it was his first lesson. He was quiet and observant
of those around him. Hurry up and wait.

At the far end of the room, Jack Mathis leaned
against a wall with his arms crossed, packet tucked
loosely under one elbow. He had already loosened his tie,
collar open, jacket slung over his shoulder like an

afterthought. He looked around with open curiosity, eyes bright, as if this were an audition he was confident he'd booked.

A sergeant passed and barked, "You. Jacket on."

Mathis grinned. "Yes, sergeant." He slipped it back on without hurry, smile never fading.

A few men nearby watched him with interest. A few with irritation.

George Axtell stood in the opposite posture entirely. He was near the center of the room, feet square, packet held in both hands as if it were something that could be dropped if not properly secured. His jacket was buttoned. His tie straight. He had removed his hat the moment he entered and now held it folded carefully under one arm, brim aligned, crease perfect.

He watched everything. He noted how long the clerks paused at certain names. How some recruits were waved through with barely a glance while others were questioned twice. He noticed the sergeant who favored humiliation over volume, and the one who used silence like a blade. Axtell absorbed the room the way other men absorbed instruction. This mattered, he told himself. All of it mattered.

Mathis caught his eye from across the room and raised his eyebrows slightly, a silent question. You see this?

Axtell did not respond. Not because he disapproved, but because he did not yet know the rules for responding.

The line advanced. Medical came next. They were herded into a long room partitioned by hanging curtains that did nothing to block sound. Boots scuffed on tiles. Men were told to strip. Some hesitated. Some joked. Jokes ended quickly.

Fred stood barefoot on cool tile, shirt folded over his arm, duffel and clothes stacked against the wall. The smell of disinfectant was sharp enough to sting.

A corpsman moved briskly, clipboard tucked under his arm, eyes efficient and bored. "Height." "Weight." "Eyes forward," he said. Fred complied.

Two stations down, Axtell stood stiffly as a corpsman checked his vision. He recited letters crisply, as if precision itself might earn favor.

Mathis, one station over, leaned forward into the eye chart, squinting theatrically.

"Relax," the corpsman snapped.

"I am relaxed," Mathis said. "That's my relaxed face."

"Step back." Mathis stepped back.

"Now read." He read perfectly.

The corpsman grunted, unimpressed.

Down the line, Charlton Ivey answered every question before it was fully asked. Hugh Russell said little, offering compliance without commentary. Douglas Lenardson's hands trembled slightly when his blood was drawn, though his eyes never left the wall. Quinton Johns joked until a corpsman told him to shut up. He did—and then couldn't quite stop smiling anyway.

Edmund Overend stood apart from all of them, expression closed, as if this were a formality he had already completed once in another life. They were weighed. Measured. Prodded. Reduced to numbers and checkmarks. Privacy evaporated.

or some, that was the first loss.

Haircuts came next. They were marched into a long room with chairs bolted to the floor. Clippers buzzed constantly, a mechanical insect sound that crawled under the skin. Men sat stiffly as years of civilian identity fell away in uneven strips, hair collecting at their feet like shed skin.

Axtell sat perfectly still as the barber worked, eyes locked on a point somewhere above the mirror. When it was done, he studied the reflection briefly, then looked away, already refusing attachment.

Mathis watched his own hair hit the floor and laughed. "That's one way to start fresh," he said.

A sergeant leaned in close. "You wanna keep that mouth, son?"

Jack met his eyes. "I was just admiring your craftsmanship, Sergeant."

The sergeant stared for a long beat, then snorted. "You'll be fun," he said. "For about a week."

By the time Fred stood, the floor was carpeted with hair. The clippers vibrated against his scalp, leaving it light, exposed. When he caught his reflection, he barely recognized the man looking back—not because of how he looked, but because of how little he felt about it. That, he realized, was new.

They were issued gear in a warehouse that smelled of canvas and oil, where a clerk gave them a stern look. "Two uniforms. One pair of boots. One blanket. Don't lose anything unless you want to buy it back with blood."

Men fumbled with unfamiliar buckles, struggled into stiff boots, cursed quietly. Axtell methodically checked each item against the list, folding his excess clothing with care even as a corporal barked at him to hurry.

Mathis shoved his gear into the duffel and slung it over his shoulder in one smooth motion. "You don't check your issue?" Fred asked quietly as they fell into step together.

Mathis glanced sideways. "I'll know if something's missing."

Axtell overheard and shook his head. "That's how mistakes happen."

Mathis grinned. "That's how you learn which one's matter." The three of them walked on without speaking further, the unspoken lines already drawn.

\#

Barracks came last. Night settled fully by the time they marched to their barracks. The building was long and low, windows open to coax air that barely moved. Inside, rows of bunks stretched wall to wall. The smell was immediate—sweat, soap, and the faint sourness of too many men in one place.

"Pick a rack," a corporal said. "You'll learn later if it was a mistake."

Fred chose one near the center, neither edge nor aisle. Axtell selected a bunk with military logic—good sightlines, proximity to exits. Mathis flopped onto the first open mattress he saw and bounced once, testing it. "Luxury," he announced. No one laughed. Men undressed in stages. Boots thudded to the floor. Socks peeled away. The sounds were intimate and anonymous at the same time.

Axtell sat on his bunk and carefully placed his folded clothes beneath it, aligning them with care that bordered on ritual. Mathis lay back with his hands behind his head, staring up at the ceiling., grin finally gone. From his bunk, Axtell stared at the ceiling, muscles tight, mind already racing ahead—standards, rankings, survival. He had come here to measure himself. The thought that he might come up short had not yet entered him fully.

Fred sat and removed the velvet pouch from his pocket. Turning it once in his hand, unseen, he tucked it beneath his pillow. Lights snapped off without warning. Darkness did not bring silence. Someone whispered a prayer. Someone swore softly. Someone laughed again, too loud, then stopped when no one joined in.

Axtell lay stiffly on his back, eyes open, already reviewing the day, cataloging errors, building improvements.

Mathis stared into the dark, feeling for the first time the shape of something he could not charm his way through.

Fred listened to the breathing around him, the unfamiliar rhythm of it, and understood that motion had finally given way to containment. Tomorrow, the sky would still be distant. Tonight, they were simply bodies in rows, strangers bound by arrival, already being shaped, the Corps already at work while they slept

Mathis was already planning how to win whatever game this turned out to be. Around them, the others lay awake or pretended not to be. Men from different roads, different assumptions, now pressed together under the same roof, subject to the same rules.

Outside, somewhere beyond the barracks, aircraft engines turned over, coughed, then settled into a low, distant growl. Fred listened until he understood the sound for what it was. Not comfort. A promise.

CHAPTER 3 – N.A.S. PENSACOLA

They moved that day from the barracks in the reception area to their school quad. The barracks smelled of dust, piss, and old sweat. It was the kind of smell that had weight on it, that seemed to cling to the back of the throat no matter how shallow the breath. Ceiling fans turned lazily overhead, their blades wobbling slightly as they tried to push warm air across rows of steel bunks and olive-drab footlockers in vain. The air didn't cool—it merely circulated, redistributing heat, humidity, and the dust of men who had already come through, those that passed and those that failed.

Boots thudded against the floor as new arrivals staked their temporary claims—top bunks, window spots, corners close to the door. The room buzzed with nervous motion: canvas scraping metal, locker lids slamming, voices overlapping as if volume itself could assert belonging.

Fred stepped inside and stopped just long enough to take it in. Order would come later. Right now, it was noise and motion. No center. No hierarchy yet—just men colliding gently, instinctively, each trying to carve out a small, defensible square of space before someone told them where they were allowed to stand.

A wiry cadet with sharp posture dropped his bag onto the top bunk nearest the window. He moved with intention, quick and economical, already assigning territory in his mind. He didn't look around to see if anyone objected. "George Axtell," he said to no one in particular. "Pennsylvania. Don't snore. Don't touch my gear."

A taller man with a relaxed grin flopped onto the lower bunk beneath him, boots still on, mattress springs protesting under his weight. "Jack Mathis. Illinois," he said. "I snore. Loud. Ain't changing." A ripple of laughter passed through the room—thin, automatic, the kind men used to keep fear contained and pointed

outward instead of inward. It rose, then died quickly, as if everyone sensed how fragile it was. Fred set his duffel on the bunk above Mathis's and offered a hand. "Fred Rauschenbach. New York." Mathis took it, grip firm, eyes already measuring, already sorting.

"You can call me J.R. Thinking I'm going to call you "NY" instead of trying to butcher that last name. Guess we'll see who makes it through."

Below the window, a man older than the rest unfolded his uniform carefully before placing it into his locker. He smoothed the fabric twice, then once more, the movements practiced, habitual. "Ed Overend. Oregon." There was no challenge in his voice, no invitation either. Just statement.

From the far side of the room, a lanky cadet with a quiet gaze raised an eyebrow without lifting his head from his locker. "Charlton Ivey. South Carolina. I'm here to fly. Not socialize."

A bespectacled young man wedged through the doorway with a stack of manuals clutched tight against his chest, nearly colliding with someone backing up. "Doug Lenardson. Michigan. Sorry," he said automatically, even though no one had spoken to him.

A broad-shouldered Georgian made his way down the aisle, shaking every hand he could reach, enthusiasm unshaken by the heat or the smell. "Quinton Johns. Georgia," he said. "I'll handle morale if y'all handle the flying."

The room didn't calm, exactly—but it settled, the way animals do when they realize they're contained.

Fred claimed his space and opened his footlocker. From the duffel he removed two small photographs: his parents standing in front of the bodega, sleeves rolled up, faces already tired, and Skid in Navy blues, squinting into sunlight on a pier Fred had never seen. He placed them where they would be visible when he lay down, then tucked the St. Joseph medallion into the corner beside them. He felt Overend's eyes linger—not curious. Assessing.

"You have family in already?" Overend asked.

"My brother," Fred said. "Submarines." Overend nodded once. "Different pressure. Same odds." Before Fred could answer, boot heels snapped outside. "Outside! Outside! Fall in! Move, move, move!"

The barracks exploded into motion again. Men scrambled for boots, for belts, for anything that made them look less wrong. Someone dropped a canteen. Someone swore under his breath. Axtell was already moving, boots laced cleanly, posture locked in. Mathis took an extra second, caught himself, adjusted. They spilled onto the tarmac in uneven rows, heat rising through the soles of their shoes. Sweat formed instantly, darkening collars, soaking armpits. Floodlights washed the world flat and white. Above them, two SNJ Texan trainers tore across the burning sky, engines snarling as they climbed. The sound cut through the formation like a blade.

Fred felt it lodging behind his sternum. This was not school. This was attrition.

That night, sleep came in fragments. The fans rattled. Someone coughed endlessly. Someone else whispered into the dark, reciting something under his breath that might have been a prayer or might have been math. Mathis snored exactly as promised, unapologetic, a steady chainsaw rhythm that drew quiet curses from both sides of the aisle. Axtell lay rigid on his bunk, hands folded neatly on his chest, eyes open. He replayed the evening in perfect sequence: the order of commands, the tone of the sergeant's voice, the moment he'd hesitated—just barely—before stepping into line. He hated that hesitation, hated that he could feel it now, magnified. Below him, Mathis slept like a man unconcerned with tomorrow. Fred lay on his back, hands behind his head, watching the shadows from the ceiling fan rotate endlessly. He touched the medallion once, then let it be.

Outside, engines coughed to life somewhere on the field, then settled back into silence. Pensacola did not sleep. It merely paused.

Morning arrived like an assault.

Lights snapped on. A whistle shrieked. A voice followed immediately, flat and practiced. "On your feet! You got sixty seconds to look alive!" Men tumbled out of bunks, collided,

cursed. Axtell was upright instantly; his boots halfway laced before his feet hit the floor. Mathis rolled, hit the concrete, laughed once, then shut it down when he saw the petty officer's face. They ran. They lined up. They ran again. The sun cleared the horizon and immediately made itself known. Heat pressed down, wet and heavy. Sweat soaked collars before breakfast. Shirts clung. Breath came shorter than it should have.

"Pensacola don't care where you're from," a chief barked as they stood at attention. "Don't care what you were. It cares what you can do today. And tomorrow. And when you're tired of doing it."

Breakfast was fast and loud. Trays slammed metal. Coffee burned. Eggs tasted like nothing. Men ate like they were being timed. Axtell counted bites. Mathis ate everything.

Later, in the classroom, chalk squealed. A lieutenant paced, pointer tapping diagrams of lift and drag. Fred felt his mind settle into familiar grooves— angles, vectors, airflow under stress. Lenardson scribbled furiously, filling pages with notes. Ivey barely wrote, eyes locked forward, absorbing. Mathis leaned back, chair tilted, listening without writing a word. "Some of you are good students," the lieutenant said. "That won't save you. Some of you think you're natural flyers. That'll get you killed."

On the flight line, heat shimmered. Engines idled. The smell of oil and fuel saturated the air. Overend stood quietly, hands clasped behind his back, eyes tracking ground crews, instructors, the aircraft themselves. "You see how they walk?" Overend murmured to Fred. "They don't hurry. They don't need to." An instructor stopped in front of them. "This place doesn't fail you," he said calmly. "You fail yourself. We just keep records."

By mid-afternoon, the line thinned. A man staggered during drills and was pulled aside. They did not see him again. Axtell's jaw tightened. Mathis noticed—and smiled, just slightly.

That night, the barracks were quieter. Not peaceful. Just subdued. Lenardson whispered equations into the dark. Johns murmured a joke that earned one tired laugh. Ivey stared at the ceiling without blinking. Axtell lay awake, muscles taut, already planning how to be better tomorrow. Mathis lay awake too, grin

gone now, staring into the dark, realizing—just beginning to realize—that charm might not be enough here. Fred listened to the building breath.

Tomorrow would begin sorting them for real. Names would give way to performance.

Performance to error. Error to disappearance.

CHAPTER 4 – THE GATES OF HELL

Noise was part of the design. It wasn't just volume. It was timing. Noise arrived precisely when silence might have allowed thought. Drill instructors filled the air with it—barking names, invented infractions, countdowns that started without warning and ended before anyone understood the rules. Whistles sliced conversations apart. Boots struck asphalt in uneven cadence as young men stumbled into formation before they knew where formation was supposed to begin or end.

The gates of the Naval Air Station loomed behind them. Tall iron bars flung wide, ceremonial in design, permanent in implication. Floodlights burned down from steel poles, flattening faces and stretching bodies into warped silhouettes. Sweat traced immediate paths down necks and backs, the Florida heat asserting itself without apology. Shirts darkened within minutes. Breath shortened. The sun had barely risen and already felt punitive.

Fred took his place automatically. He did not remember stepping forward. His body had learned the rhythm faster than his mind. Stop. Align. Stand still. Someone near the far end of the line shifted too late.

"Feet together. TOGETHER." The correction echoed off concrete and metal alike.

This gate had another name. It wasn't official. It didn't appear on maps or paperwork. But instructors used it, and cadets learned it quickly. The Gates of Hell.

Axtell stood two men over, posture immaculate, chin lifted just enough to read as discipline rather than defiance. His eyes were fixed forward, unblinking, jaw locked as if tension itself were armor. Mathis stood looser by comparison, rolling his shoulders subtly, working tension out of his body the way a man prepared for a fight he half expected to enjoy. Lenardson adjusted his glasses, then caught himself and froze, hands at his sides, embarrassed by the reflex. Johns scanned the line with open curiosity, already cataloging faces, instincts clashing with nerves. Overend didn't move at all. Not even to blink.

A chief paced slowly in front of them, boots clicking deliberately out of rhythm. He stopped. He barked, finger snapping out. "Eyes forward. This isn't sightseeing." Johns snapped to attention a half beat late. "Yes, sir." A flicker of a smile crossed his face and vanished instantly.

The chief stepped close enough that Johns could smell coffee and tobacco on his breath.

"You find something funny, son?" "No, sir." "Good. Keep it that way."

They were marched inside at a pace designed to disrupt breathing.

The doors slammed shut behind them with a finality that landed somewhere below the ribs. The classroom smelled of chalk dust, sweat, and overheated wiring. Ceiling fans rattled uselessly. Chairs scraped as men found seats— too fast, too slow, too hesitant. Every choice was wrong until proven otherwise. At the front of the room stood a first lieutenant whose face looked carved rather than aged. His eyes were tired, not bored. The difference mattered.

"Figley," he said. "Some of you will remember my name. Most of you won't." Silence stretched. "That'll depend on how you fly." No one wrote yet. "Flying," Figley continued, "is the easy part. Surviving is not." He turned and pulled down a chart. It crackled loudly.

The lesson consisted of dates, aircraft types, weather conditions, altitudes, and names of the men lost in training. Not in combat. Not overseas. No enemy involved. Just gravity, weather, machinery, and error. Figley did not dramatize it. He didn't need to.

Captain Hayes took over then, broader shoulders, heavier voice, less grace. "Eight dead this year," he said flatly. "At this station alone." A chair creaked. "That's more than one a month. Pilot error. Weather. Equipment failure. Pick your poison." The fans chopped at the air overhead.

"They were smart," Hayes continued. "Educated. Motivated. Some better than you." He let that land. "They just believed they were ready."

Fred felt Mathis stiffen—not physically, but ideologically. A shift that said challenge, not fear. Axtell's jaw tightened hard enough to jump. Lenardson's pencil never stopped moving.

"How many of you think you won't wash out?" Hayes asked. No hands. "How many think you shouldn't?" Nothing. "That's good," Hayes said. "Overconfidence kills faster than gravity."

#

Outside again, the heat felt heavier. The tarmac radiated it upward, cooking them from below while the sun blazed down from above. Cadets jogged until their formation dissolved, then were shouted back into shape. Mistakes were public. Corrections were louder. Names became weapons. One man stumbled during a pivot and caught himself with a hand on the ground.

"Wrong answer," an instructor snapped. "Drop." The man dropped. "Down. Up. Down. Up."

His arms shook by the tenth repetition. Sweat pooled beneath his chest. No one moved to help. No one looked away. Water breaks were brief and supervised.

Johns leaned close to Mathis, voice low. "Whole thing feels like they want us to quit. "They do," he said.

"Some of us should," said Axtell.

Mathis bristled. "And you figure you're not one of 'em?"

Axtell turned then, eyes level. "I figure I don't make mistakes." The silence afterward had weight.

Fred saw it clearly now: this wasn't rivalry yet. It was a difference in worldview. Axtell believed precision could conquer all variables. Mathis believed instinct could outrun them. Lenardson trusted preparation. Johns trusted people. Overend trusted nothing he hadn't already survived.

Flight training would test every one of those beliefs.

\#

The second classroom was worse. Smaller. Hotter. No windows. A different instructor this time—Lieutenant Commander Shaw—thin, sharp, impatient.

"You don't learn to fly here," Shaw said. "You learn whether you deserve to."

Shaw followed up by drilling them on systems, fuel starvation, carb icing, dead-stick landings. He taught them about emergency procedures at a pace the class found overwhelming. But even as they floundered, Shaw went after them with rapid-fire questions and made note of any hesitation.

Lenardson answered two in a row, voice tight but correct. The third answer stuck. Shaw waited. Lenardson tried again. His voice faltered. "Sit down," Shaw said flatly. Lenardson sat, face burning. Axtell answered the next question flawlessly.

Mathis didn't raise his hand. He watched instead, sizing up his instructor, tracking cadence, tone, and motive. Shaw stopped in front of him. "You. Why didn't you answer?"

Mathis shrugged slightly. "Didn't need to."

Shaw leaned closer. "That confidence will kill you."

Mathis met his eyes. "Only if I'm wrong."

Shaw smiled without warmth. "We'll find out."

That afternoon, they were taken to the flight line. They saw their training birds, the Stearman NS-1 "Yellow Peril".

A slow moving biplane with few instruments and a very forgiving plane which made it ideal for training.

Figure 2. Boeing-Stearman NS-1.

Aircraft sat baking under the sun, oil streaking their fuselages, propellers still and lethal. Instructors walked them past wreckage—bent aluminum, twisted struts, scorched panels dragged to the side like carcasses.

"No ceremony," one instructor said. "Just reminders." Lenardson slowed near one wreck, staring too long. "Keep moving," the instructor snapped. Lenardson swallowed and obeyed. Overend said nothing. His eyes flicked once to a cracked canopy, then away. Fred felt the medallion warm against his chest.

That night, the barracks felt heavier. Not quieter. Just compressed. Mathis sat on his bunk, boots off, forearms resting on his knees. "They want us scared," he said quietly.

"They want you accurate," Axtell replied.

"They want you obedient," Mathis shot back.

Axtell stood. "Obedience keeps you alive."

"No," Mathis said. "Judgment does."

The room stilled. Other men pretended not to listen. Fred watched both, understanding that this argument would not end here. Lenardson lay awake, staring at the ceiling, whispering checklists until his voice cracked. Johns stopped joking. Overend lay still, already somewhere else.

Outside the fence line, surf broke steadily against the shore—indifferent, repeating without error or mercy. Tomorrow they would be ranked. Evaluated. Separated. The Corps didn't care who liked whom. It cared who adapted. The gates behind them were already closing.

Stand-To

No whistle. No warning. Just lights snapping on at 03:47 a.m. and a voice tearing through the barracks like shrapnel. "UP. UP. UP." Men came out of bunks tangled in sheets, disoriented, some already on their feet before they understood where they were. Someone fell. Someone cursed. A metal locker slammed hard enough to ring. "Outside in sixty seconds. You miss it, you pay."

Fred was upright immediately, boots half-laced as he stood. The room was chaos—fabric tearing, canvas scraping, bodies colliding in the narrow aisle. Axtell was already dressed, movements sharp and silent, teeth clenched as he tightened his belt. Mathis rolled off his bunk, landed light on his feet, blinking sleep from his eyes as he pulled on his shirt. Lenardson fumbled, glasses slipping from his fingers. He caught them just before they hit the floor, hands shaking more than he wanted anyone to see.

Outside, the air was cooler but thick with moisture. The sky was still black, stars dulled by coastal haze. The men formed up badly spacing off, lines crooked. A chief walked the line slowly.

"Count off." The count started strong, then fractured. "Seven—eight—ten—"

"STOP." The chief stepped forward, his face unreadable. "You skipped nine."

A man near the middle blurted, "Sir, I—"

"Drop." The man dropped.

"Everyone drop."

They hit the asphalt together. The surface was cool but unforgiving. Palms burned. The man who'd miscounted breathed hard almost immediately. "Down. Up. Down. Up."

Fred counted silently. So did Axtell. Mathis stopped counting after ten and focused on rhythm. Lenardson lost the count and panicked, correcting himself twice, breath ragged.

"This isn't punishment," the chief said conversationally. "This is calibration.

Get your defecation in sequence!"

By the time they were allowed up, shirts were soaked again. The sky had lightened by a shade. No one had gone back to sleep.

#

They called it a flight physical.

It felt like a sorting room. They moved through stations in silence. Vision charts. Hearing tests. Reflex checks. A white-painted corridor that smelled of antiseptic and old fear.

Fred stood barefoot on cold tile while a corpsman checked his pupils. "Any dizziness?"

"No."

"Nightmares?"

"No." The corpsman nodded, made a mark, waved him on. Axtell passed through like a machine, every answer precise, every response measured.

The doctor glanced at his chart twice. "You ever panic?"

"No, sir."

The doctor raised an eyebrow. "Everyone panics."

Axtell met his eyes. "I manage variables."

The doctor wrote something Fred couldn't see.

Mathis leaned back in the chair during his exam, too relaxed.

The corpsman noticed. "You don't seem nervous."

Mathis shrugged. "Should I be?"

"You're here."

Mathis smiled. "So are you." The corpsman didn't smile back.

Lenardson's screening took longer. He answered everything correctly. Too quickly. Too completely.

"Slow down," the doctor said gently. "Take a breath."

Lenardson nodded, inhaled, exhaled. His hands trembled anyway.

"You ever freeze under pressure?"

"No, sir."

"You ever feel overwhelmed?"

"No, sir." The doctor waited.

Lenardson swallowed. "I ... I prepare."

The doctor made a longer note this time.

Down the hall, a man came out of a room pale, eyes unfocused. Two petty officers flanked him without touching him, guiding him away as if he might break. No announcement. No explanation. Just subtraction. Fred watched the door close behind them.

\#

The barracks were mostly quiet. Not asleep—just subdued. Fred lay on his bunk, eyes open, listening to the building breathe. Somewhere down the row, Lenardson whispered procedures under his breath, voice barely audible, like a charm against collapse.

Mathis sat on his bunk, elbows on his knees, boots unlaced but still on. He stared at the floor for a long time before speaking. "You really believe that" he said.

Axtell didn't look at him. "Believe what?"

"That if you're perfect, you'll survive."

Axtell turned slowly. "I believe mistakes kill people."

"So does freezing," Mathis shot back. "So does hesitation. So does pretending the world stays inside the margins."

Axtell stood. He was careful with it, like every movement mattered. "You think this is about feeling? You think instinct saves you when the engine quits at five hundred feet?"

"I think thinking too long gets you killed," Mathis said. "I think flying's a conversation, not a formula."

Axtell shook his head. "That's how amateurs talk."

Fred watched them, understanding something settle into place: neither of them was wrong. Neither of them was safe.

Axtell spoke again, quieter. "People like you rely on luck."

Mathis leaned in. "People like you don't know when luck's already gone." They stood there, breathing hard, until footsteps approached. Both stepped back instantly. The moment didn't resolve. It calcified.

CHAPTER 5 – SUMMER KILLS

Summer arrived without warning.

One week it was tolerable. The next, the air settled over Pensacola like a weight that did not lift. It did not announce itself with drama. It simply stayed. Heat climbed off the tarmac in visible waves, turning distance soft and deceptive. Engines ran hotter, gauges creeping upward in increments small enough to ignore until they weren't. Tempers shortened. Mistakes crept in quietly, often unnoticed until they compounded. By June, fatigue was its own constant.

Despite the heat, training continued as before. Days began before the sun burned clear of the horizon. Men woke up covered in sweat. Briefings blurred into flights, flights into debriefs. Sweat soaked through uniforms before engines even turned over. Water was rationed by common sense rather than instruction, which meant it was never enough. No one complained. Complaint required energy. The instructors adjusted nothing.

"Summer kills," one of them said once, conversationally, after grounding a cadet for sloppy procedure. "Every year." Fred heard it. Remembered it. In the air, the margin thinned.

\#

The first real warning came not with an accident, but with fog. It rolled in low over the bay, early and quiet, blurring the horizon into something that looked harmless from the ground. From the air, it erased reference. The sky and water merged into a pale, undifferentiated sheet that offered no depth, no distance—only the illusion of safety until you were inside it.

Fred led a routine formation hop. Nothing complicated. Familiar aircraft. Known voices. He felt settled as the wheels lifted, the vibration smoothing out as the SNJ Texan climbed. Controls. Airspeed stabilized. The usual transition from ground noise to airborne clarity took place—except the clarity never fully arrived.

"Two, check in."

"Two."

"Three."

"Three, tighten up," Fred said, keeping his voice level. *"Come left two degrees."*

No answer. Fred adjusted immediately, banking shallow to widen spacing, buying time. He didn't wait for confirmation. In formation flying, waiting was how errors multiplied.

Mathis slid in without being asked, easing closer to the drifting aircraft, voice calm. *"Three, look at my wing. You're good. Just hold that."*

The SNJ steadied. A fraction at first. Then more.

Fred held the formation until the fog thinned enough to regain horizon. They completed the hop without further incident.

After landing, the instructor only said, "Good catch back there."

Fred shrugged. "That's why he's on my wing." Mathis pretended not to hear it. But he did. Fred meant every word.

\#

The heat deepened. By mid-June, preflight inspections felt like endurance trials. Metal burned through gloves. Fuel fumes hung heavier in the air. Men drank water until their stomachs sloshed and still felt dry. The first crack showed itself on a clear morning, the kind instructors favored. No weather to blame. No excuses to hide behind.

The Gulf lay flat and blue beyond the runway, heat already lifting in faint waves. Trainers waited nose to tail, engines ticking as ground crews finished checks. Fred walked the line with the others, helmet tucked under his arm, listening without appearing to. Axtell moved ahead, focused, eyes already somewhere beyond the aircraft. Mathis joked with Johns, volume a shade too high, laughter just a little forced. Lenardson lagged half a step, running mental checklists even as the real ones were being called. They were no longer strangers. That was the danger.

In the briefing shack, the instructor laid out the drill—formation turns, spacing discipline, emergency break procedures. "Today we fly clean," he said. "Not fast. Not brave. Clean."

Axtell nodded once. Mathis rolled his shoulders. Lenardson swallowed.

In the air, the difference between them widened. Fred felt himself settle as the wheels lifted free of the runway. Controls responsive. Noise resolving into something usable. He held position easily, neither leading nor chasing, watching the others through small corrections of stick and throttle. Mathis pushed closer than necessary, tightening the formation, riding the edge of proximity like it was proof of confidence. Axtell held line with mechanical precision, no drift tolerated, corrections minimal and exact. Lenardson hovered between them, correcting too often, always a half second late.

"Ease it," Axtell snapped over the radio. "You're crowding."

"I've got it," Mathis shot back.

The instructor cut in. "Maintain spacing. Both of you."

They turned into the sun. Glare washed the canopies white. Lenardson's aircraft dipped unexpectedly—not much. Just enough. Fred banked away instinctively, increasing separation as the formation broke.

"Who lost altitude?" the instructor demanded.

Lenardson answered too quickly. "I—corrected for wake."

"By guessing?" Axtell said.

The instructor took control and brought them down without comment.

On the ground, silence did more damage than shouting. Lenardson failed his check ride that afternoon. The examiner cited delayed decision-making. Excessive correction. Loss of situational awareness under pressure. The words were clinical. Accurate. None of them felt cruel. Lenardson accepted the critique with a nod, face drained of color.

When the room cleared, he remained seated, staring at a diagram he had drawn the night before. Fred found him there. "You froze," Fred said gently.

Lenardson nodded. "Because I didn't want to be wrong."

Fred understood. Wanting to be right had nearly gotten them all hurt.

That evening, the barracks held a tight, electric quiet. Mathis lay on his bunk, boots off, staring at the ceiling fan. "Guy flies like a textbook," he said. "But this isn't a test."

Across the room, Axtell sat rigid, gear aligned to regulation. "And this isn't a circus," he replied. "One mistake kills everyone."

The words landed hard and stayed there. Fred let them sit.

Later, when the lights dimmed, Fred pulled paper from his footlocker and sat on the edge of his bunk. The fan whirred overhead, constant and indifferent. He wrote slowly.

> *Dear Skid,*
> *We've started flying*
> *together now. You can see who*
> *trusts instinct and who trusts*

He folded the letter and slid it into his locker beside the medallion. Tomorrow someone else would fail. Or worse, someone would not walk away.

#

Fred's landing was clean. Wheels touched down in sequence, tires chirping once before settling. Fred taxied clear, ran post-landing checks without thinking, followed the marshal's signals into line. Engines idled down. Canopies opened. Heat rushed in immediately, thick and unrelenting.

Inside the briefing shack, helmets came off. Sweat-darkened flight suits clung to skin. Someone joked about finally nailing a turn radius. Someone else complained about glare on final. The instructor waited until everyone was seated. He closed the door. "Before we go over tomorrow's flights," he said evenly, "you should know we lost a man this morning." The room adjusted in small, involuntary ways. "Cadet Second Class Walter Emmons. Advanced class. Instrument phase." Fred felt the words settle—not shock. Weight. "He flew into terrain during a low-visibility approach. Controlled flight. No mechanical failure." Silence took shape. "He was six weeks from wings."

Then the instructor opened the flight log. "Let's continue." They did. But every correction now had a face.

The service came the next morning. Uniforms pressed. Sky too blue to cooperate.

The chaplain did not dramatize it. "Training losses," he said. "The phrase sounds administrative. It isn't."

The coffin sat at the front, flag-draped and precise. Fred watched Emmons's classmates in the front pews— faces rigid, eyes forward, as if memorizing themselves. "He died learning," the chaplain said. "Because learning to fly takes place on the edge of failure."

\#

Summer finished its work. Washouts accelerated. Names disappeared. Empty bunks stayed empty. By August, even instructors stopped commenting. Flying changed. Less talk. Less bravado. Controls felt heavier. Movements economical. Enthusiasm burned away, leaving competence.

By September, the heat broke. Fred realized he had crossed another line. Summer had killed the excess. What remained was readiness.

CHAPTER 6 – SOLO

Fred learned he would fly solo the same way most things happened at Pensacola—quietly, without ceremony, buried inside a routine that offered no room to argue. The weather board showed clear skies and light winds, a rare kindness that felt almost accidental. The instructors moved down the line with clipboards tucked under arms, checking names, scanning readiness the way machinists checked tolerances. No one smiled. No one lingered.

When Figley stopped behind him, Fred knew. "You're up," Figley said. "One circuit. Don't make it interesting."

"Yes, sir." There was no handshake. No encouragement. No pause to let the moment register. Figley moved on immediately, already assessing the next man, the next risk.

Fred stood for a second longer than necessary, letting the words settle—not as excitement, not as fear, but as fact. Solo. The word had weight now. It had crossed from concept into schedule. Around him, the morning moved on as if nothing had changed. Ground crews worked through their routines. Engines coughed, caught, then settled. Somewhere down the line, another instructor raised his voice, correcting a cadet's posture as if posture still mattered.

Mathis met Fred's eyes from three aircraft over. No grin. No thumbs-up. Just a slight lift of the chin. About time. Axtell didn't look at him at all.

The walk to the aircraft felt longer than usual. Fred carried his helmet under his arm, the sound of engines rolling across the field in steady waves. Heat rose early, the October sun already leaning toward punishment. The SNJ Texan waited exactly where it always did, sun-bleached, metal warm to the touch, oil streaks etched permanently into its skin.

Figure 3. SNJ-1 Trainer.

Nothing about it suggested this flight would be different. That was the point.

He circled the aircraft slowly, forcing himself not to rush. Tire pressure. Control surfaces. Fuel caps. He laid a hand flat against the fuselage for just a second longer than required, feeling vibration even before the engine turned over.

He climbed in, strapped down, and ran the checklist aloud. "Fuel selector—on. Throttle—cracked. Mixture—rich." His voice sounded steady in the headset. He didn't trust that yet.

The instructor leaned over the cockpit rim, listening without comment, one hand resting casually on the canopy frame. "You know what to do," Figley said at last. "The airplane will tell you the rest." Then he stepped away. That was it.

The canopy came down with a muted thud. The world narrowed. The edge of the field disappeared behind curved glass. Fred advanced the throttle and felt the aircraft surge forward, lighter without a second body, more responsive, eager in a way that felt almost unsettling.

Taxiing felt different immediately. Less resistance. Less inertia. The nose responded faster to pressure. He compensated without thinking, years of habit already adjusting.

At the hold-short line, he paused. Not because he needed to. Because he wanted a pause.

He brought the engine up, checked the mags, and watched the gauges stabilize. Everything was green. Everything was normal. He rolled onto the runway.

The throttle went forward smoothly. The engine roared. Acceleration came quicker than expected. The nose lifted sooner than his body anticipated. For a fraction of a second, the ground hesitated. Then it released him. He was alone.

Not abandoned. Not exposed. Simply alone in a way that left no buffer between action and consequence. No voice beside him. No hand hovering near the controls. No one corrected a misjudgment before it became real. The burning sky opened cleanly and accepted him. The SNJ climbed willingly, lighter now, obedient. Fred trimmed carefully, feeling the aircraft settle into balance. Every correction traveled directly through the airframe, unanswered by another voice, unchecked by outside hands. His breathing slowed.

Around the pattern, the field curved beneath him, familiar and newly strange. Buildings looked flatter. Distances stretched. Angles sharpened. Without an instructor beside him, the world felt both simpler and less forgiving. He thought of Lenardson—of freezing not because he didn't know, but because he knew too much.

He pushed the thought away. Airspeed. Bank angle. Spacing. Flying had never felt this honest.

Below him, another aircraft faltered. Fred saw it out of the corner of his eye as he came around the downwind leg—a wobble, slight but wrong. The nose dipped, corrected too hard, then dipped again. An instructor's voice snapped over the radio, sharp and immediate. "Ease it. Ease it. I've got you."

Fred held his line, eyes forward, heart rate unchanged. This wasn't his problem. It couldn't be. The aircraft recovered and continued. The pattern absorbed it without comment.

On base leg, Fred resisted the urge to rush. The runway filled the windscreen faster than expected. He adjusted early, trimming gently, letting the aircraft come to him instead of forcing it. Final approach felt long. Too long.

He forced himself to trust the numbers. Altitude. Speed. Sink rate. He flared earlier than instinct wanted and held it there, hands light on the stick, letting the aircraft decide when it was done flying. The wheels touched down with a brief, forgiving chirp.

He rolled out smoothly, heart pounding now—not from fear, but release.

Taxiing clear of the runway, he felt the weight return—not physical, but contextual. The sky gave him back to the field. Engines idled down. Canopy opened, heat and noise rushed in immediately, reclaiming him. Figley stood waiting near the edge of the tarmac.

"Well?" the instructor asked.

Fred shut down the engine, removed his helmet, wiped sweat from his brow.

"Normal," he said. Figley allowed himself to make the smallest nod.

"That'll do."

No handshake. No praise. The clipboard came up. A checkmark appeared.

Another risk cataloged.

Fred watched two more solos that day. One went clean. Quiet. Forgettable in the best way. The other didn't.

The cadet flared late, overcorrected, bounced hard, then tried to salvage it instead of going around. The instructor took the controls just in time. The aircraft taxied back without incident. The cadet didn't look at anyone.

By afternoon, the word had spread without being spoken. Solo was no longer theoretical. It was happening. Men carried it differently—some louder, some quieter, all aware that this line could not be crossed twice.

Back in the barracks that night, no one made a show of it. Mathis clapped Fred once on the shoulder. "About time." Lenardson asked about trim settings. Specific. Technical. Safe.

Axtell listened from his bunk, arms folded, expression unreadable.

Later, the adjutant burst in to demand signatures for a new maintenance log procedure no one had time to follow. Groans rippled through the room. The kind of bureaucratic interruption that felt obscene after flying alone. Fred met Mathis's eyes across the room. Same conclusion: this is idiocy of the highest order. They said nothing until the room cleared.

Mathis sat on the edge of a bunk, rubbing his face. "Someday that regulation's going to save us."

Fred raised an eyebrow. "Save us from what?"

Mathis smirked. "From thinking anyone up the chain knows what they're doing."

Fred laughed once—quiet, brief, the kind only Mathis ever seemed able to coax out of him. Axtell watched from his bunk, jaw tight. "Procedures exist for a reason," he said.

"So do instincts," Mathis replied. The argument didn't start. It didn't need to. It was already alive.

That night, when the lights were out and the fans turned overhead, Fred lay awake longer than usual. The sky had not judged him. It had simply responded. He thought of Skid beneath the surface of the Gulf, trusting steel and pressure, trusting training to hold when instinct couldn't. Different elements. Same laws. Tomorrow, others will fly alone. Some would falter. Some would not.

Fred reached for the medallion around his neck, held it briefly, then hung it in his locker.

Solo did not mean free. It meant accountable.

CHAPTER 7 – GOLD WINGS

February 1941

February cooled the field without ceremony. The heat receded enough that breath no longer felt borrowed. Jackets appeared again in the mornings. Engines turned over cleaner. Pensacola looked almost forgiving beneath winter light. Graduation did not arrive as a single moment. It unfolded in sequence—paperwork, briefings, signatures—the administrative mechanics of becoming something else.

By midmorning, they were no longer cadets. They stood in formation on the parade ground in dress uniforms, posture altered by necessity rather than pride. The line was shorter than it had been in spring. No one commented on it. Counting was unnecessary.

The colonel stepped forward and spoke without flourish. "Effective 10 February 1941," he said, "you are commissioned officers in the United States Marine Corps Reserve. Second Lieutenants, your status changes. Your obligation deepens."

There was no pause to let it settle. "You are no longer here to be evaluated," the colonel continued. "You are here to be trusted. That trust will be tested immediately."

Names were called. Each man stepped forward in turn, received his commission, and accepted the rank without gesture. Gold bars replaced uncertainty. Gold Wings followed soon after. When Fred's name was spoken, he moved automatically. The insignia felt lighter than he expected, its meaning heavier. The wings were pinned below the bars—a visual equation he would need to understand quickly. An officer. A pilot. No longer insulated by training status.

No longer buffered by excuse.

"Well done, Lieutenant," the colonel said quietly. Fred saluted, nodded once, and returned to the line.

Afterward, the new second lieutenants gathered in loose knots across the field. Mathis grinned as though he had outrun something invisible. Lenardson turned his wings over in his hands, tracing the edges, verifying weight and finish. Axtell examined his bars once, then fixed them in place with mechanical precision. Johns laughed a little too loud, relief escaping before he could restrain it. The absence stayed with them. Empty places where men should have stood—no longer cadets, never officers.

The formation had been adjusted to hide the gaps. It failed. A photographer organized them anyway. History tended to record what remained, not what was lost.

CHAPTER 8 – BUTTERBARS

Dear Skid,
I was commissioned today. Second Lieutenant.
They pinned wings on me as if the two things were interchangeable. I don't think they are. One means you can fly. The other means people will follow you, whether you deserve it or not. They stopped calling us cadets this morning.
The word disappeared all at once. No one asked if we were ready.
I know you understand that part.

Fred sealed the letter and placed it in the Out Box.

Night settled over the base, cooler now, cleaner. The barracks felt altered— not quieter, just aware of itself. Men moved differently. Voices carried a fraction more authority, even when joking. The word *lieutenant* hung in the air, unused but present. Fred sat on his bunk with the locker open, the medallion resting in his hand. Gold Wings and gold bars caught faint light together— symbols forged from months of endurance, not celebration. Tomorrow, orders will scatter them. Different Squadrons. Different roles. Responsibility without rehearsal. Fred fastened the wings back onto his uniform, then the bars. They did not make him safe. They made him accountable.

Figure 4. 2Lt. Fred Rauschenbach, 1941.

CHAPTER 9 – HOLDOVERS

1941

Orders did not come. The group expected them to arrive immediately. Envelopes, names, destinations. The machinery of reassignment clicking into motion now that wings and bars had been pinned. Instead, days passed. Then a week. The parade ground returned to routine, the sense of transition suspended midair. They were no longer cadets. They were not yet anything else.

The notice appeared on the board outside Operations, typed and unsigned.

**TEMPORARY DUTY ASSIGNMENT
INSTRUCTOR PILOTS
PENDING REASSIGNMENT ORDERS**

Figley gathered them that afternoon in a bare classroom with the windows open just enough to let sound through—engines taxiing, props winding up and down. "You're holdovers," he said. "Which means you're useful and inconvenient at the same time." A few smiles surfaced and were gone.

"You've survived the syllabus," Figley continued. "That doesn't make you instructors. It means you won't kill someone by accident. The distinction matters. You'll fly with new cadets. Demonstrations only. Pattern work. Emergencies. You'll correct mistakes before they become reports. If you don't, you'll answer for it."

Mathis leaned back in his chair, arms crossed, the confidence of someone who finally knew the rules. Lenardson leaned forward, already attentive. Axtell asked one question.

"Who signs off for us?" Figley met his eyes and smiled. "Me, for now".

\#

Over the next weeks they taught theory in the classrooms, and practical application in the skies. They flew constantly. Hands light. Eyes sharp. The authority came awkwardly at first. Cadets overcorrected when spoken to. Froze when corrected too late. Fred learned quickly that tone mattered as much as timing. "Anticipate," he said once, sharper than intended. The cadet nodded, eyes wide, grip tightening. Fred adjusted. "Let the airplane tell you what it needs."

The days acquired a suspended quality: waiting layered on top of work. Speculation circulated quietly— fleet squadrons, carriers, specialty tracks. No one said combat aloud, but it hovered anyway, just beyond the edge of conversation. Europe burned closer with each passing bulletin. The Pacific tightened. At night, the barracks felt transitory. Men arrived. Men vanished. Names disappeared from the board without comment.

They were pilots. They were officers. They were not yet assigned. Holdovers. Soon enough, that holding would end.

CHAPTER 10 – THE DISRUPTOR

The ready room door opened inward. At first, only light entered. Then a man.

First Lieutenant Gregory Boyington did not bother to look like an instructor. His cap was pushed back too far. His collar sat open, regulation ignored just enough to be intentional. He moved with the loose confidence of someone who no longer needed to announce credibility. There was a faint smell of aviation fuel and tobacco about him, as if both had followed him inside.

Boyington stopped just inside the room and scanned the faces without comment.

Figley gestured once with his chin. "This is First Lieutenant Greg Boyington, transferred in from San Diego," he said. "He signs for you now." A few of the men straightened automatically.

Boyington's mouth twitched—not quite a smile. "Don't look so relieved," he said. "I sign the paperwork. Gravity signs the test." He leaned back against the desk, arms crossed.

"You're holdovers," he continued. "Means someone thinks you're good enough not to waste and cheap enough to keep around. Congratulations."

Mathis grinned despite himself. Boyington's gaze snapped at him. "You think this is funny?"

"No, sir."

"Good. Because teaching someone else to fly is how most pilots discover what they don't know." He paced once across the front of the room. "You will not show off. You will not improvise. You will not try to look impressive in the rear seat. If one of your cadets kills himself, you'd better go down with them—or you'll answer to me before you meet your maker." He stopped in front of Fred. "What's your name?"

"Rauschenbach, sir."

"Where are you from?"

"New York, sir."

Boyington nodded once. "Then that's what I'll call you. NY. You ever been shot at?"

"No, sir."

"Neither have I," Boyington said. "But I've buried enough pilots to know enthusiasm doesn't travel well at speed. Just enough to ruin your life if you screw it up," he said. "And just enough to save someone else's if you don't." The room absorbed that.

Boyington did not brief them the next morning. He walked straight from Operations, his helmet already under his arm, and they followed him to the flight line.

"NY," he said without looking back. "You're with me." Fred fell in.

"You ever see an airplane lie to someone?" Boyington asked, resting his hand on the cowling.

"No, sir."

"Good. It doesn't. People do."

In the air, Boyington flew harder than the syllabus allowed—but never sloppily. He showed edges manuals avoided. Recovery points that were not labeled. He let the aircraft drift just far enough to make the lesson unavoidable, then corrected cleanly.

"You freeze, you die," Boyington said calmly over the radio. "You rush; you die. Precision and competence live in between." On final approach, he bled altitude deliberately. "Most pilots die close to the ground," he said. "They think the hard part's over." They landed smoothly.

Back on the line, Mathis pretended not to stare. Lenardson asked nothing. Axtell watched differently now—less judgment, more calculation. Boyington handed Fred his helmet.

"You fly clean," he said. "Don't let the books convince you that's the same as flying safe." He paused. "Don't let confidence turn into ego. They look identical from 10,000 feet." Then he walked away, already lighting a cigarette he shouldn't have been smoking.

Fred rested a hand on the aircraft. The airplane was unchanged. The margins were not.

Figure 5. Cadet Gregory Boyington, 1936.

CHAPTER 11 – DOWN TIME

Spring 1941

Normalcy arrived quietly. The work settled into a rhythm that felt almost reasonable. Flights in the morning. Pattern work before the heat climbed too high. Debriefs finished by midafternoon. Maintenance wrapped early enough that evenings belonged, briefly, to no one. They got weekends off. No one trusted that at first.

On Friday afternoons, the flight line thinned sooner than expected. Hangar doors slid closed. Engines went quiet. Someone put a radio on near the barracks, its signal drifting in and out with the wind. Life beyond the fence line pressed closer. Some of the men found company nearby.

Pensacola offered girls who worked in cafés and bookstores, nurses with shore-leave smiles, daughters of shop owners who treated pilots as something between novelty and promise. First names were exchanged easily. Last names rarely mattered until they did.

Mathis danced badly but enthusiastically, laughing when his feet betrayed him. Johns played to crowds instinctively, his charm landing where effort was applied. Lenardson attended gatherings cautiously, never quite at ease, though attentive. Others sent letters and watched calendars.

Girlfriends arrived from the north. Fiancées stepped off trains in summer dresses, clutching overnight bags that carried hopes not yet tested. Introductions were careful. Affection kept public but restrained. When operations allowed, Skid sent letters that were brief, controlled, and unmistakably distant.

BBQs appeared near the enlisted quarters, and near the summer holiday weekends, smoke hanging low while someone played a harmonica badly. Beer was iced expertly, shared carefully, always with an eye toward the morning's checklist. Laughter came easier when tomorrow looked predictable. There were picnics beyond the base perimeter—blankets spread beneath scrub pine, engines far enough away to forget. Conversations drifted in easy directions: future jobs, places to return to, futures imagined without precision.

One Saturday night, under a full moon, someone suggested swimming. They slipped past the outer fence in civilian clothes, boots abandoned in a pile. The water was warm and forgiving, moonlight turning skin silver and sound indistinct. Female laughter carried across the dark, brief and unguarded. Fred floated on his back for a while, listening to voices blur into something manageable. No engines. No commands. Just water and breath. It felt earned.

CHAPTER 12 – FLY LIKE AN EAGLE

Boyington taught them things no one else did. He taught them by flying badly on purpose, at angles and speeds that made the aircraft feel uncooperative, almost offended. He showed them what the plane did when the pilot hesitated, then what happened when the pilot committed too late. He talked less than Figley, corrected later than Axtell, and trusted instinct where others trusted margins.

"Stop flying the book," he said once, leveling out after a recovery that sat well outside the syllabus. "Fly the airplane."

Fred watched the way the room shifted when Boyington entered it. Instructors leaned forward. Cadets stared. Men who had already earned wings found themselves being re-graded without warning. Boyington even made Figley listen.

Boyington flew with Mathis and proved that aggression needed shape. He flew with Lenardson and forced him to act before certainty arrived. He flew with Axtell and didn't correct him at all.

Afterward, Axtell stood in silence, replaying the flight like a problem that resisted solution.

"You didn't tell me what I did wrong," Axtell said.

Boyington smiled thinly. "No, I didn't," he said.

"Why not?"

"Because you already know. You just don't want to fly that way."

Teaching the teachers worked. Accident reports dipped. Pattern work tightened. Cadets recovered faster and froze less. Instructors began borrowing Boyington's language when speaking to students—talk of edges, timing, commitment. The results were undeniable. But so were his violations.

Boyington drank like a man unconcerned with witnesses. He drank off base, then on it. He drank with enlisted men, even though he shouldn't have, and with officers who outranked him but pretended not to notice. He gambled openly. Dice behind the hangar. Cards in quarters with the doors half open. He won often enough that resentment followed him like smoke.

Minor infractions stacked neatly into thick folders. The sergeant major kept count. "This man's going to get himself court-martialed," he said once, watching Boyington walk across the field with a cigarette already lit.

"Yes," Figley replied. "But not before he gets someone else home alive." Fred saw it coming apart in pieces.

One afternoon, Boyington arrived late to a briefing, eyes clear, uniform rumpled beyond tolerance. Figley stopped the session cold. "You've got charges pending," Figley said evenly.

Boyington shrugged. "I always do."

"You want to keep flying here?"

"I want to keep flying," Boyington said. "Anywhere."

That was the truth of it. Rumors followed. Warnings quietly delivered, reprimands softened by necessity. But eventually, he was faced with charges. Even though Europe's skies were full now, and the Pacific was tightening daily, the Corps did not tolerate misbehavior. Certainly not in public anyways.

In June, Fred found him alone on the edge of the flight line just after sunset, staring at a parked aircraft with something like affection. "You teach like you're leaving us," Fred said.

Boyington didn't look over. "I am."

"Orders?"

Boyington smiled without turning. "Eventually." He flicked ash into the wind. "They'll tolerate me as long as I'm useful," he continued. "They'll excuse me as long as I'm right. After that—" He shrugged. "Uniform doesn't change the man."

"That doesn't bother you?" Fred asked.

Boyington finally turned. "No," he said. "Dying stupid bothers me."

By late summer, the paperwork would reach a point where it could not be ignored. The numbers were too clean. Boyington's violations were growing too visible, while tolerance thinned. Boyington's lessons remained, though his continued presence could not.

CHAPTER 13 – WING AND A PRAYER

The briefing room was full before anyone said why.

Maps were already pinned to the boards—the Mediterranean rendered in flat colors, Crete outlined in red grease pencil. Photographs followed: shattered stone, collapsed olive groves, gliders splintered across fields like thrown matches.

The intelligence officer spoke without drama. "May twentieth," he said. "German airborne operations during the invasion of Crete." He tapped a photograph with a pointer OPERATION MERCURY. "DFS 230 Gliders".

Figure 6. DFS 230 German Glider

Towed in low. Released early. Silent insertion. Troops landed directly onto objectives—airfields, supply routes, command nodes.

"No engines. No warning. With adequate opposition," the officer said. "Heavy casualties . . . successful none-the-less."

The room adjusted. Fred watched instructors lean forward. Pens stopped moving. Every man present understood what silence meant in warfare—not absence, but surprise.

"They lost nearly forty percent of their airborne force," the officer said. "But they took the island."

A murmur rippled and died quickly. "The Germans considered the casualties to be acceptable." That was the line that stayed. Acceptable. What mattered, the officer explained, was not the survivability of the aircraft. It was arrival of its cargo. Objectives seized before defenders could respond. Surprise purchased with certainty.

Afterward, Figley stood alone at the front of the room. "Everyone seems to think gliders are a novelty," he said. "Europe just proved otherwise." He glanced down the rows. "The Marine Corps will not be last to learn this lesson."

"They landed on top of the fight," Mathis said. "No engines. No second passes."

Lenardson nodded grimly. "One chance."

The photographs stayed on the board after the briefing ended. No one rushed to remove them. Outside the room, the conversation fractured.

"They died on schedule," Mathis said quietly. "That's what bothers me."

"It's not bravery," Lenardson replied. "It's design."

Axtell studied the map longer than necessary. "It removes indecision."

Fred thought of Boyington's voice—don't rush, don't freeze. Of submarines slipping beneath the surface with no engines and no second thoughts. Different machines. Same margins.

From then on, gliders crept into his lessons
without announcement. Not as doctrine. As emphasis.

CHAPTER 14 – RESIGNATION

Summer pressed in hard. Training cycles continued. Cadets arrived wide-eyed and left narrowed by experience—or absence. The instructors remained. Boyington's influence lingered in the air even as the man himself unraveled on the ground. By July, the stories stopped being rumors. Dice games behind the hangars turned ugly. A fistfight in town left a broken window and a bruised civilian jaw. Boyington's tab at a local bar became an open secret, his debts carried by men no longer willing to carry them. Everyone knew. No one was surprised.

Fred said nothing.

By August, Boyington stopped pretending to manage the balance. He drank hard and openly. He gambled when sober enough to win and fought when he wasn't. Reprimands followed him like punctuation marks he chose to ignore. The Corps tolerated many things. Debt was not one of them. His decision came quietly. Boyington resigned his commission.

Not in disgrace—not officially—but with relief thinly masked as opportunity. A path out that spared court-martial and preserved utility elsewhere. China was accepting volunteers. Civilian contracts. The First American Volunteer Group, the "Flying Tigers," were fighting. The group consisted of fighter squadrons of around 30 aircraft each that trained in Burma before the American entry into World War II to defend the Republic of China against Japanese forces. The AVG were officially members of the Republic of China Air Force. The group offered contracts with salaries ranging from $250 a month for a mechanic to $750 for a squadron commander,

Boyington made the choice himself. "I'm not built for waiting," he told Figley. "Or fences." Figley didn't argue.

The farewell was just a gathering near the edge of the flight line as the sun dropped low enough to soften the heat. No speeches. No orders read. Men stood in uneven shade while Boyington packed a bag that looked too small for what he was carrying with him.

"You headed for glory?" Johns asked.

Boyington snorted. "I'm headed for pay."

Mathis shook his hand anyway. Lenardson hesitated, then did the same. When Boyington reached Fred, he paused.

"You fly clean," he said again, as if finishing a sentence begun weeks earlier. "That'll keep you alive. Just don't confuse clean with careful."

Fred nodded.

"When you see Skid again," Boyington added, "remind him submarines and airplanes obey the same god."

"Gravity?" Fred asked.

Boyington smiled. "Commitment." Then he was gone.

By September, the season shifted. Mornings started to cool. Jackets returned. Cadets continued cycling through as if Europe and the Pacific were concepts rather than coordinates.

They were still instructor pilots. Still teaching. Still waiting.

Fred wrote less now. Not from detachment, but because Skid's silence had stretched into something heavier than explanation. He understood operational quiet. He understood doctrine. But understanding didn't ease the weight of it.

One night, Fred sat on his bunk with the medallion resting in his palm. St. Joseph of Cupertino—patron of flight, of impossible lift. Gliders needed no lift once released. Only accuracy. Boyington had chosen a sky without rules. Skid lived beneath an ocean defined by them. Fred remained where he was—between orders, between answers, between margins.

He realized then what Boyington had been. Not a role model. Not a warning. A stress fracture. A visible fault line showing where the structure would fail when pressure exceeded tolerance.

War would test it soon.

The instruction continued. So did the waiting. Both were teaching him what acceptable really meant.

CHAPTER 15 – SILENT ARRIVAL

The Marine Corps did not copy the Germans. It translated them. There was no appetite for mass airborne infantry dropped inland to seize territory. That was an army problem, and a risky one.

Marines thought in terms of arrival under fire, not of occupation. Of putting force exactly where it would matter, exactly once, and holding long enough for reinforcement to arrive by sea or air. Crete did not teach them how to land. It taught them when the landing mattered. Instructors began reframing familiar problems. Approaches were discussed not as patterns, but as commitment arcs. Points beyond which correction no longer existed. Silence was no longer an absence to be avoided, but a condition to be managed.

"You don't announce yourself," Figley said during one such lecture. "You appear." Maps changed. Beaches replaced runways. Distances were measured not in miles, but in seconds of exposure. Every approach assumed hostile observation. Every landing assumed the first wave would absorb losses for the second. The Marine answer to gliders was not romance—it was control. If silence was required, it would be mechanical: engines throttled low, profiles flattened, gliders following each other into landing zones. Stacked tight, they felt unsafe until they weren't. If sacrifice was required, it would be carefully calculated, with aircraft expendable, pilots not.

"You don't ride in on faith," Boyington said once from the back of the room. "You ride in on math you trust." No one contradicted him.

The emphasis shifted subtly but permanently. Training flights now included no-go recoveries—points at which aborting was treated as failure, not prudence. Cadets were taught to recognize the last moment before commitment, then act without hesitation. Axtell absorbed this cleanly. "Once you decide," he told a student, "You stop evaluating."

Mathis adapted differently. He learned to delay instinct until it mattered, then let it go completely. Lenardson struggled but improved. Silence no longer means uncertainty— it means sequence.

Fred recognized it immediately. It was the same logic as submarines. Same as gliders. Same as Boyington's flying on the edge. The airplane would not save you once you crossed the line. Only judgment could. The Corps did not announce this shift. They never did. It simply became the way things were taught.

By late summer, the word Crete was no longer spoken aloud. Its lessons were already embedded—silent arrivals, irreversible decisions, margins calculated before wheels ever left the ground. When the time came, Marines would not drift into battle. They would soar.

CHAPTER 16 – WINGS OF ANGELS

August 1941

It happened on a clear day. That was what unsettled everyone afterward—the absence of an explanation. No weather. No mechanical failure. Just two aircraft occupying the same airspace, closing faster than awareness could correct. The sortie was routine: instructor pilots flying with cadets on navigation exercises over familiar ground. Spacing liberal. Altitude adequate. Radios quiet enough to lull attention.

Fred was offset to the right, scanning his sector, when a transmission cracked across the frequency—sharp, incomplete. "*TRAFFIC!*"

The word tore off mid-syllable. Fred rolled hard, eyes searching instinctively. He saw the convergence then—two trainers crossing at a shallow angle, both correcting simultaneously, neither one enough. There was no violence in the contact.

No explosion. Only the grinding refusal of metal to share space. A wingtip shredded. A strut folded. One aircraft lurched upward and rolled. The other snapped downward, already losing authority. "Mayday, mayday!!" came a voice Fred recognized but could not place in time.

\#

Axtell's aircraft shuddered, then flattened into a sickening spin. Altitude fell away in tight, unforgiving rotations. Fred followed at a distance, powerless to intervene. "Bail out!" someone shouted into the open channel.

For a moment, nothing happened. Then a dark shape separated from the aircraft. A parachute blossomed late but clean—white silk snapping open just as the trainer disintegrated into the trees below. Fred tracked the canopy as it drifted, absurdly gentle against the green.

There were no other chutes. Axtell's student cadet remained with the aircraft until impact.

The other plane never recovered. It vanished behind the tree line in a steep arc, engine screaming until it didn't. All three men were killed instantly. The burning sky went quiet again.

Cadet James Arnold Mitchell
Cadet William F. Poe Jr.
Cadet William S. Wampler

Axtell hit hard and was recovered by a ground crew an hour later. Minor injuries. Bumps and bruises. Shaking hands. Blood on his sleeve where silk had burned his palms. He did not speak.

The debrief avoided names at first. Two aircraft. Three fatalities. Successful bailout.

Cause Undetermined would be entered cleanly into the report—language stripped of judgment but not weight.

At the memorial service, three coffins rested at the front, flags tight across their contours.

Axtell stood at the rear. His uniform was perfect. His face was not. The chaplain spoke carefully. About decision-making under pressure. About recovery opportunities that arrive unevenly.

When the service ended, no one approached Axtell at first. Finally, Mathis did, then stopped short and chose not to speak. He embraced Axtell in an attempt to shift some of the weight he was carrying. Fred stood nearby, watching the man who had trusted precision more than anyone else now bear something no system could compute.

That night, Fred wrote but did not send the letter.

Skid,
Three men died today.

Fred folded the paper and placed it beneath the medallion in his locker. Skills had not failed them. Training had not failed them. Timing had. Timing, like war, did not negotiate.

Summer pressed on. New cadets arrived. Engines turned over. The airspace reset itself.

Axtell returned to the flight line days later, quieter, carrying knowledge the syllabus did not cover. Everyone who flew with him afterward felt the margin narrow—not in him, but inside themselves.

CHAPTER 17 – WEDDING BELLS

Fall 1941

Axtell's return to the flight line changed things in the flight duty. He did not speak about the jump. No one asked him to. The knowledge traveled without language—in quieter briefings, in the extra pause before a maneuver, in the way men looked at one another when a checklist was complete and still didn't guarantee anything. Three men were gone. One continued.

It settled over the instructors like a low-pressure system. No one framed it as fear. That would have been inaccurate. What took hold instead was urgency, the realization that your existence was provisional, that skill postponed endings but did not always cancel them. Men began thinking forward.

Weekends filled faster. Letters were written with more intention. Introductions became purposeful. What had once been companionship now carried weight. Legacy stopped being an abstract word. Girlfriends became fiancées.

Fred married first.

He married Ellen Engstrom in September 1941. They stood before a minister who spoke clearly about commitment as an act of will. There was no orchestra, no extended reception. Just hands joined with the knowledge that separation would arrive on a schedule neither of them controlled. Fred wore his dress uniform. The wings felt heavier now. The bars more real. When they spoke the vows, he felt the unfamiliar weight of being seen—not as a role, but as a promise.

Afterward, the couple walked along the water in silence, shoes in hand, the sound of waves doing what waves always did. "Will this change anything?" Ellen asked.

Fred considered it. "Yes," he said. "It will give everything else somewhere to land."

Quinton Johns made his choice loudly. Christmas leave became an engagement party, which became a wedding that felt closer to a celebration of survival than a formal rite. Laughter outweighed solemnity. He wanted witnesses.

Hugh Russell waited longer, then married with determination sharpened by time. Charlton Ivey did the same. The irony was not lost on anyone when the two scheduled weddings for the same weekend pass: different states, different chapels, the same impulse.

Axtell followed. He moved carefully now—but decisively. His ceremony was small, deliberate, structured like everything else he did. He stood straighter than usual, as though daring the universe to argue with him again.

Douglas Lenardson was the last. His wedding was precise down to the minute, vows spoken with the same earnest seriousness he brought to flight planning. He looked relieved afterward, as if finally committing to something without needing to second guess.

Over the months, Fred watched it unfold with quiet understanding. Comrades returned to base wearing rings—exhausted, but unmistakably steadier.

CHAPTER 18 – ANCHOR POINTS

Not everyone followed the same path. The "Boys" gained a new comrade in arms, **Lieutenant Richard "Dick" Day**. He had been a line officer for years. Cuba. Ground billets. Experience without altitude. One day, he decided to fly.

As a student, he caught Mathis's eye. Mathis took him on quietly, correcting without ceremony, trusting him early. Day earned his wings later than most, but once he did, he joined the holdovers whenever he could—and fit in as if he'd always been there.

Mathis, Day, and Overend remained unapologetically unmarried. They attended every wedding. Shook every hand. Toasted with genuine warmth. They danced when asked and left when it suited them

"Someone's got to keep one foot loose," Mathis said once, half-smiling. "In case the ground gives out." No one argued.

As days turned into weeks and weeks into months, rings caught light in ready rooms and cockpits. Photographs appeared inside lockers, tucked beside checklists and regulations. Names are spoken differently now. Fewer jokes. More care. Marriage did not make them braver.

It made them deliberate.

When Axtell flew, men noticed the way he checked airspace—not obsessively, but completely. When Fred took the air, Ellen's face sometimes arrived uninvited at altitude —not as distraction, but as calibration. They were still instructors. Still flying daily. Still watching the world tighten beyond the horizon. But now, when they climbed into aircraft or sat through evening briefings, the stakes were no longer theoretical.

Each man had drawn a line between existence and meaning and chosen to anchor something on the far side of it. Wedding bells did not drown out the sound of engines. They gave them context.

As 1941 moved toward winter, the boys understood something without saying it aloud:

Whatever came next would more than just interrupt life. They were playing a game they couldn't walk away from.

CHAPTER 19 – PROJECT GEORGE

Boyington's departure left a big hole. Everyone wondered what the future would bring. Early one morning, they arrived to find a hint. The name appeared before any explanation.

PROJECT GEORGE BRIEFING: Rm 202

It was written on the chalkboard in Operations one morning, block letters pressed hard enough to leave dust impressions behind. Conversations slowed when men saw it. Waiting had taught them that names mattered more than speeches. The briefing was closed and secured.

Maps stayed rolled. Photographs and charts remained covered until everyone was seated.

"The Marine Corps as you know has been studying silent delivery," the intelligence colonel said. "Not as theory. As a logistical and somewhat tactical strategy." No one needed to ask where the idea had come from. Crete still cast a long shadow, its arithmetic unresolved.

"Gliders," the colonel continued. "Short-field insertions. Precision landings. Units arriving intact and unnoticed." He paused deliberately. "Seizing objectives and holding them until follow on units arrive." "This will not be experimental flying," he said. "This will be controlled risk."

First Lieutenant Figley passed out the envelopes. He moved down the row deliberately, name by name, placing each packet directly into waiting hands. There was no ceremony to it—only the quiet precision of a man who understood that movement mattered more than anticipation.

"Do not open them yet," Figley said.

The envelopes rested lightly. Deceptively thin. Figley returned to the front of the room and waited until every man had settled. "Now." Envelopes opened almost in unison.

Fred read his first line, then the second. Temporary Assignment—*Project George. Headquarters: Quantico, Virginia.*

Around him, reactions appeared and were quickly mastered. Russell nodded once. Lenardson reread his twice. Johns allowed himself a brief smile. Mathis grinned openly, already thinking in terms of distance rather than location. Ivey folded his orders with measured satisfaction. Six men. One project.

#

Axtell's envelope differed. He read it once and slipped it cleanly into his breast pocket.

Naval Academy—Annapolis, Maryland. Post graduate studies in Meteorological Engineering. Precision applied to education.

"Well," Axtell said lightly, "looks like back to school for me, fellas. Headed to the Academy. I'll see you in the soup soon enough."

Before anyone could respond, Figley cleared his throat. "I also have new orders."

The room recalibrated instantly. "I've been promoted to Captain," Figley continued. He did not pause. "And I've accepted command of Project George." That landed heavier than the envelopes.

"I will be accompanying those of you assigned to Quantico," he said evenly. "Effective immediately, I am your commanding officer."

Fred felt the alignment lock. Whatever Project George was becoming, it would not drift.

"Between glider duties," Figley continued, "you will be assigned ferry work throughout the continental United States, based on the needs of the Corps." Different aircraft. Different routes.

No routine. "You'll design, test, and fly gliders," Figley said. "But you'll stay current. You'll go where I tell you, when I tell you."

Project George was to be staffed by men who had lived through instruction, attrition, loss, and delay—men who understood commitment not just enthusiasm.

\#

Overend stood only after the others finished reading. He had not received an envelope. "I'm not taking an assignment," he said. The room shifted. "I'm the oldest one here," Overend continued evenly. "And I won't spend the next year preparing for a war I can already join." No one interrupted.

"I've resigned my commission," he said. "I'm going to China." Someone exhaled.

"Flying Tigers," Mathis said quietly.

Overend nodded. "Boyington's already there. Someone needs to keep him from getting himself killed." There was no laughter.

Later that afternoon, Fred walked the flight line alone. Trainers traced familiar patterns above ground that felt subtly different now, as if their purpose had shifted without their knowledge. Pensacola had been a place of formation. Now it was a point of divergence. At dinner, conversation returned to the topic at hand.

"Quantico's our headquarters," Johns said. "Means planning, not glory."

"Damn, gliders." Lenardson replied.

"Means figuring out how not to die before the landing—during, or after," Mathis added.

Fred thought about arrival again. About silence. About committing without correction. It feels like standing at the edge of something that hasn't been named yet. Mathis smirked "They won't know what hit them when the six of us arrive."

By the end of October, movement resumed across the base. Six men prepared to head north. Axtell to Annapolis. Overend west, toward China and risk without regulation. Fred, Mathis, Russell, Johns, Lenardson and Ivey were all headed to Project George.

"Dick" Day was staying on at Pensacola. Pensacola would continue doing what it always had—training men for futures it could not predict. Project George would replace waiting with intention. The boys were no longer holding.

They were being aimed.

\#

Winter 1941—Joliet, Illinois / Quantico, Virginia

The Marine Corps did not announce its experiments the way civilians expected. There were no headlines. No speeches. No claims of innovation meant for public consumption. There were only orders—thin envelopes, stamped and signed, delivered without context and accepted without questions. That was how Project George entered execution.

At Quantico, they were assembled without ceremony: pilots, engineers, instructors, and men whose records suggested adaptability rather than seniority. Fred recognized the pattern immediately. The Corps was not looking for stars. It was looking for men who would work inside uncertainty and not complain when the ground shifted beneath them.

Figure 7. LNS-1 Glider towed by Jeep.

They called it Marine Glider Group 71. The concept was simple enough on paper—gliders, towed silently into combat, landing men and equipment where boats and parachutes could not. What the paper did not account for was terrain. Or weather. Or the reality of landing something fragile into a place that actively wanted to kill it.

#

At the Lewis School of Aeronautics in Joliet, Illinois, the work began in earnest. The Corps sent its newest glider specialists to a civilian school. Gliders were not flown so much as managed. They demanded patience over aggression, judgment over instinct. Lift was earned rather than forced. Every landing was a negotiation with gravity—and gravity always demanded payment.

Figure 8. LNS-1 Glider being towed through the air.

Fred liked the discipline. So did Russell. Johns absorbed it quietly. Lenardson asked better questions than most engineers. Ivey never pretended it would be easy. Mathis treated it like a problem meant to be solved, not conquered.

They learned tow-plane dynamics. Release altitudes. Sink rates under load. What happened when gliders landed intact—and what happened when they did not. They crashed often enough that wreckage became instructional rather than alarming. The Corps observed and recorded everything. Reports were filed. Modifications ordered. Then more reports.

\#

At the Naval Aircraft Factory in Philadelphia, prototypes came apart and went back together again. Engineers discussed survivability with professional detachment, though no one could ignore what the numbers implied. In controlled conditions, gliders worked. In combat, they invited a level of exposure no

doctrine could fully justify. Still, they pressed forward.
That was the Marine Corps way.

Joliet felt strange—more fraternity house than
military post. The fields outside town lay flat and brittle
under winter skies. Gliders rose reluctantly into cold air,
released, then slid earthward in long, patient arcs that
rewarded precision instead of aggression. It was quiet,
cerebral flying. Angles. Airspeed. Lift without power.
Judgment without margin. The kind of mistakes that
announced themselves only after it was too late to correct
them.

CHAPTER 20 – INFAMY

December 7th, 1941

The day began like all the others. Coffee drank too quickly. Hands stiff in gloves. Breath clouding inside hangars while mechanics worked without commentary. The war existed somewhere else—on maps, in newspapers, in speeches no one here had time to listen to carefully.

After lunch, someone turned on the radio. It was meant as background—music, perhaps a weather update—but the voice cut through the room with a tone that arrested everyone without instruction. *". . . Japanese aircraft have attacked Pearl Harbor . . ."*

Fred felt the silence before he understood the words.

Russell stopped midway through fastening his jacket.

Johns turned slowly, as though sudden movement might shatter something fragile.

Mathis stepped closer to the radio, hand rising unconsciously as if to steady it.

Lenardson leaned against the workbench, color draining from his face.

Ivey did not move at all.

" ... ships burning ... aircraft destroyed on the ground ... casualties still uncounted ..."

No one spoke. The voice spoke to us. They listened as the broadcast cut away, returned, repeated itself—because the nation itself did not yet know what to say next.

Fred looked around the room. They had all known, abstractly, that war was coming. Europe was aflame. Asia had been burning for years. But this. This was not preparation anymore. Their war had arrived.

\#

By midafternoon, the civilian school changed texture. Phones rang without pause. Officers gathered in knots that broke and re-formed. Orders were not issued so much as anticipated. Training continued—but under a new gravity. As if every movement were now being recorded for judgment later. The Marine Corps shifted instantly. No confusion about purpose. No debate about intent. Whatever the Corps had been preparing for had arrived, irrevocably.

Fred felt it settle not as anger, but as clarity. They would not be glider pilots forever.

They would not remain instructors. They would not stay behind. This was no longer a question of if, or even when. It was how soon.

That evening, they sat together in silence longer than usual. Nobody needed to say what came next. Mathis finally broke it. "Well," he said carefully, "that settles it." Russell nodded once. Johns stared into his coffee as if it might offer a solution. Lenardson exhaled, slow and measured. Ivey said only, "Them sons-of-bitches." Fred didn't speak.

He thought instead about what the Corps would ask of them. Not theory, not innovation, not careful experimentation, but execution. Speed. Endurance. Men willing to accept incomplete preparation and impossible demands without hesitation. They were already doing that. They just hadn't realized it yet.

The next morning, a glider lifted again into the cold December air, released, and descended silently.

Training for a kind of war that no longer existed. None of them watched it land.

They were each lost in their own thoughts.

CHAPTER 21 – GLIDER GROUP 71

January 1942—Parris Island, South Carolina

The first thing Fred noticed after finishing at the Lewis School of Aeronautics was the silence. Not the productive quiet of concentration, but the absence of expected news. Skid's letters had stopped entirely now—not spaced out, not delayed—simply gone. Fred understood the logic of it. Submarine operations erased predictability by design. Understanding did not ease the unease. Silence carried weight when it persisted long enough.

He carried it with him into Project George's next incarnation.

The unit's name appeared on paperwork almost overnight: MARINE GLIDER GROUP 71, Marine Glider Squadron, 711. Fred was assigned as Assistant Engineer Officer. It was not a role he had imagined for himself, but it fit. The war had already begun sorting men into places they had not anticipated.

By 1942, theory had hardened into numbers. Requirements replaced concepts. Prototypes took shape at the Naval Aircraft Factory in Philadelphia—utilitarian structures stripped of romance. Wood. Fabric. Cable. Aircraft designed to arrive intact and expend themselves without argument.

Fred split his time between Quantico, Parris Island, and NAS New York. He moved constantly. Slept lightly. As Assistant Engineer he helped design planes, learned to speak in tolerances and margins measured against inevitability. The factory floor smelled of lacquer and sawdust rather than oil and exhaust. He walked beneath skeletonized wings, traced joints with gloved hands, asked questions that lived one layer beneath optimism. How does it fail? Where does it flex? What breaks first?

The same questions and answers could describe his so-called marriage. Ellen hadn't seen him since he left on his assignment, and she was beginning to complain.

Figure 9. Two pilots inspect LNS-1 Glider.

Fred was promoted to **First Lieutenant on 28 February 1942**. Responsibility arrived without ceremony. He signed more documents. Answered for more decisions. Slept no better. The test glider developed a reputation—unstable, underpowered, temperamental in crosswinds. No one wanted to take it up that morning. Fred scanned the roster, then folded the clipboard under his arm.

"Mathis," he said. "You're flying the evaluation."

Mathis didn't blink. "Copy."

An enlisted man whispered later, "Why him? That crate's cursed." Fred answered without hesitation. "If it goes wrong, he won't freeze."

Mathis overheard this time. He said nothing, but Fred saw the acknowledgment in the nod—an understanding between two men who would trust each other with worse soon enough.

Fred was promoted to **Captain on 7 August 1942**. The bars felt different now. Less symbolic. More procedural.

Figure 10. Marine pilot stands next to N3N-3 plane used to tow.

CHAPTER 22 – A PATH NOT TAKEN

In November of 1942, Marine Glider Squadron 71 moved west to MCAS Eagle Mountain Lake, Texas. Parris Island had grown too crowded for glider operations. The landscape changed, and testing continued, but the questions about glider performance capabilities and risks as a military strategy did not. He recorded the results. Gliders arrived intact, but too often, the conditions required to make them useful did not. Tow aircraft were vulnerable. Release points unforgiving. Landing zones were ideal only on paper. Men could survive. Equipment could be delivered. Against an enemy waiting with artillery, mortars, and machine guns? They would not.

Ferry "milk runs" filled the gaps—short hops up and down the East Coast, longer legs inland and back again. The Atlantic appeared often now, steel gray and waiting. Fred wrote when he could. Still hoping to hear from Skid.

By early 1943, Fred was back in Philadelphia again, testing revisions that grew increasingly academic. The war was moving on without them. Amphibious doctrine refined itself in blood. Carrier aviation proved decisive. Helicopters—once dismissed outright—began appearing in briefings with uncomfortable persistence.

The glider concept did not fail. It simply no longer mattered. The end came quietly. No stand-down formation. No acknowledgment of effort wasted or lessons learned. Orders would be issued. Personnel reassigned efficiently. Project George was never declared a mistake, just a path not taken.

The six Boys gathered one last time beside a glider that would never fly again, its fabric taut, its frame still clean. Mathis ran a hand along the leading edge. "Shame," he said—not sentimentally.

"Would've been something." Russell shrugged. "The Corps doesn't need something. It needs what works." Fred nodded. The Marine Corps did not mourn abandoned ideas. It took what it could use and moved on. The men would need to do the same.

But sometimes, years later, Fred would remember the gliders: the silence of them, the way mistakes announced themselves slowly. That, he understood, had been the real training.

CHAPTER 23 – LOUD ARRIVAL

Spring 1943

By March, the tone changed definitively. They gathered one evening without ceremony. Just pilots who had moved together long enough to recognize the sound of endings. "So," Johns said finally, "what comes after arriving quietly when no one wants quiet anymore?" "Jets are coming," Lenardson said after a moment. "Transports are improving. Ground troops want certainty, not elegance." Mathis leaned back. "Figures. We spent two years perfecting something nobody wants."

Fred thought of Skid. Of silence stretched thin by time and depth. Of gliders committed without engines and submarines committed without air. "Whatever happens," Fred said, "we weren't wrong. Just early." No one contradicted him.

Outside, engines cycled through the night—louder, heavier, unwilling to disappear.

War demanded presence now. Speed. Overwhelming arrival. Fred stood later by a factory window, rain beading on the glass. Somewhere beneath the ocean, Skid lived by the same faith in design and preparation. Somewhere ahead, the Marine Corps would decide where men like him were most useful.

\#

Fred already suspected what he'd be flying next. There was one aircraft the Navy didn't quite trust— overpowered, temperamental, difficult to land on carriers. The F4U Corsair. Within weeks, he would be learning a machine that demanded aggression instead of restraint. Power instead of patience. The Corsair did not glide into anything. It arrived loudly. Decisively. With consequences.

The rumors had already arrived. They traveled faster than the aircraft itself. Everyone knew the Corsair before they saw it—or thought they did. They knew the statistics, the headlines, the slogans handed down by instructors who had never yet trusted their lives to it. They knew it was powerful. They knew it was fast. They knew it had frightened the Navy badly enough to keep it off carriers longer than intended.

But what they knew and what stood outside on the ramp were different things. The F4U Corsair was not elegant. It was long-nosed and hunched, its inverted gull wings bent downward and then up again like a bird of prey bracing itself before striking. Its thirteen-foot propeller looked less like propulsion than threat. It dwarfed the men walking beneath it, demanded clearance and respect before it would even turn. This was not a trainer. This was not forgiving. The Corsair did not tolerate weakness.

Fred followed the reports as they circulated through Quantico and Philadelphia through late 1942 and into early 1943. He read combat write-ups from the Pacific, maintenance notes, pilot impressions etched in margins. He immersed himself in data because the Corsair demanded mastery without hesitation, unlike the gliders that demanded commitment without recovery.

Fred stood with Mathis and the others he had invited to a demonstration around the first aircraft they would soon be expected to master. Russell studied the wing roots. Lenardson was already thinking structurally. Johns watched the landing gear with quiet suspicion. Ivey said nothing at all. No one reached out to touch it.

The airplane had been designed around an engine first and a pilot second. The Pratt & Whitney R-2800 Double Wasp sat forward like a clenched fist, two rows of cylinders generating more than two thousand horsepower. Everything else—fuselage, wings, pilot— existed because the engine required it. It was the first American fighter capable of sustaining more than four hundred miles per hour in level flight. It was also perfectly capable of killing its own pilot if mishandled.

Figure 11. F4U Corsair.

The **Ensign Eliminator** is what the Navy called the F4U Corsair. Not as an insult, but a warning. Visibility over the nose was poor. Torque on takeoff was vicious. Landings demanded absolute discipline. Stall behavior punished hesitation. The Corsair did not forgive indecision.

But in the air—once it was flying the way it wanted to fly—it became something else entirely. Designed to kill the Zero, it was its executioner. The Zero could turn tighter. That advantage vanished the moment the Corsair refused to turn at all. Instead, it climbed away under power the Japanese fighter could not match, rolled faster than anything it fielded, and dove like gravity itself had taken sides.

Tactics changed because the airplane necessitated a change in fighting tactics, including speed, climbing, diving , and tight turning. The trend was toward more boom and zoom, altitude as armor, but speed above all else. At that 400mph there would be no more turning fights, no more romantic ideas of maneuvering. The Corsair taught them to strike, disengage, climb, and return. When it returned, it brought enough ordnance to reshape the ground war:

Six .50-caliber machine guns fed by hundreds of rounds.
Five-inch HVAR rockets.
Twenty-millimeter cannons.
Two thousand pounds of bombs when needed.
Napalm when the war required even more ugliness.

The Corsair could hunt aircraft in the morning, hammer armor at midday, and claw infantry out of caves by afternoon. That versatility saved lives: sometimes the pilot's, sometimes the men on the ground who never learned the pilot's name.

Fred came to understand the Corsair not as a weapon, but as a contract. It would give you everything it had if you respected it. It would betray you instantly if you did not. Pilots learned its habits quickly, the way the engine talked when it was tired, the way the airframe vibrated before something failed, the exact moment when a landing ceased being salvageable. They learned to believe in it without wholly trusting. The plane was unforgiving. Cantankerous? Pilot error. Plane by plane performance differences? You could fly 1 plane today and a different one tomorrow that would perform unexpectedly. Maintenance crews praised the Corsair and cursed it in equal measure. It demanded constant care and repaid it with survivability that bordered on arrogance. It came back riddled with holes, trailing oil, missing control surfaces—and still landed. Sometimes.

By the end of the war, the Corsair would earn a kill ratio exceeding eleven to one: for every Corsair lost, eleven enemy aircraft were shot down. The Corsair achieved that impressive ratio not because it was gentle or forgiving but because it required discipline to become lethal. Pilots would fly many aircraft in their service.

None would feel alive the way this one did. None would carry into memory with the same weight—the sound of the engine at full power, the smell of oil and cordite in

Figure 12. Corsair production line, Connecticut.

the cockpit, the knowledge that every return was conditional. It was Fred's job to make sure his pilots never forgot that.

Japanese pilots named it before they fully understood it: Whistling Death.

The sound came as the Corsair dove or turned hard, air screaming through its intake ducts, metal announcing arrival seconds before impact. Survivors

would later say the sound mattered more than the sight—
warning you could hear but not outrun.

Project George was dying quietly now, starving by
shifting priorities and louder solutions. The Marine Corps
no longer needed silent arrival. Project George would be
cancelled officially by the summer of 1943. The Corps
needed air superiority over contested islands and close
support where distances collapsed into minutes and
meters. Fred wanted the Corsair. Not abstractly. Not
academically. He wanted to fly it.

Fred would get his chance. He received orders for
MCAS Cherry Point. Executive Officer, VMF-321.

CHAPTER 24 – VMF-321 (OJT)

VMF-321 did not waste time on introductions.

The Corsairs were already there when Fred arrived—dark blue hulks lined with purpose, scarred from training sorties that treated mistakes like debts with compounding interest. Work-ups and on-the-job training began before dawn and ended whenever the aircraft said they were finished. Schedules existed only to be overrun. The airplane decided when a day was done.

Fred learned the squadron by pattern and rhythm. Cold engines coughing awake in the half-light. Checklists recited without flourish or superstition. Curved approaches flown exactly as briefed—or punished immediately. These landings were not graded; they were survived.

As Executive Officer, Fred's authority lived between margins. He was close enough to the line to feel the aircraft's temper, far enough back to see patterns forming—who rushed, who hesitated, who learned fast, and who learned loudly. He flew when he could. When he wasn't flying, he observed from the edge of the runway or the back of the ready room, filling legal pads with short, unsentimental notes.

The Corsair demanded command, not persuasion.

The squadron learned to give it what it wanted.

The first losses occurred during training. They included a bent landing gear, a prop strike that stopped just short of flipping a bird into the dirt, and a pilot that froze high on final and muscled the airplane instead of committing to the wave-off. The Corsair responded exactly as designed. Fred grounded him without drama. Two weeks later the man flew again—better. Quieter.

Others did not get that second chance.

His time as XO was measured in weeks.

On 20 May 1943, Fred's reassignment orders arrived: **Navigation Officer, Headquarters Squadron 32, MAG-32.**

On paper it read like a lateral move. It wasn't. Headquarters work widened his horizon brutally. Fred moved from squadron problems to group realities—routing, timing, fuel consumption, risk distributed across formations instead of individuals. Weather stopped being something you flew through and became something you planned around days in advance. Enemy action entered calculations without warning. He flew less but thought more.

When a situation exceeded his authority, he escalated it cleanly and stepped back without resentment. Ownership, he learned, did not mean control. It meant accountability.

By June, the war accelerated its demands. Men were needed where cohesion had to exist before arrival. Leadership stopped being something you practiced and became something you were expected to bring already formed. On 1 July 1943, his new orders came without preface. His orders followed close behind: **MCAS Cherry Point, Commanding Officer, VMF-322.** He requested just one thing... Major Jack "J.R." Mathis.

CHAPTER 25 – COMMAND

July 1943 Cannonballs

MAG-32 was reorganized. Fred's promotion to **Major, effective 9 May 1943**, arrived without ceremony, justified by responsibility rather than ambition. The bars felt procedural now—tools rather than milestones. Fred was to activate and command a new Corsair fighter squadron. VMF-322. The Cannonballs. Fred stood alone in an empty office and read the orders twice, overwhelmed by the scope of the assignment: Commanding Officer. Thirty-two F4U Corsairs. Eighteen officers. One hundred eighty-nine enlisted men.

The rank did not change his reflection in the glass. What changed was the silence afterward—the moment when nothing more needed to be decided, only accepted. Command did not ask if he was ready. It asked how he would proceed. Fred folded the paper. Square it on the desk. Reached for his cover.

Outside, engines were starting somewhere on the field, the sound of power being turned into purpose. Fred left the office to find Mathis. It was time to build a squadron.

The Corps didn't argue. Mathis arrived days later, grinning like a man walking into a bar fight he had already decided to win. "Gunnery Officer?" Mathis asked. "Best one I know," Fred replied. Mathis ran a hand along the Corsair's wing root, reverent despite himself. "She's ugly," he said.

"She's honest," Fred answered.

They learned the airplane together—its torque on takeoff, the way it rolled hard if disrespected, the climb that felt indecent when the throttle came forward. The Corsair didn't lift so much as ascend, pulling pilots into vertical regimes that dared comparison. Fred understood it fully during his first extended flight. The airplane did not want to be managed. It wanted to be commanded.

Landing became predictable once flown properly. It required curved approaches, disciplined air speed, and commitment throughout each flight. The same lessons gliders had taught, now delivered with horsepower and teeth. Nothing in Project George had been wasted. Commitment points mattered. Arrival mattered. The Corsair simply arrived with guns on.

That night, Fred wrote Skid:

> *"I've found the airplane*
> *I should have been flying all*
> *along.*
> *It doesn't forgive*
> *mistakes. I think that's why I*
> *trust it."*

The Marines had found their weapon. Fred had found his place.

Somewhere far across the Pacific, men who heard the whistle would soon learn what it meant: The fight had arrived.

\#

"The boys had landed well." That was how Figley put it once, half to himself, when the postings finally settled. It wasn't praise. It was recognition—pilots scattered by necessity, arriving intact on the far side of ambition, luck, timing, and the needs of the Corps.

By the summer of 1943, the assignments told a story no one could have planned.

Major Frederick "NY" Rauschenbach assumed command of VMF-322 as a twenty-three-year-old. Responsible for a Corsair fighter squadron still forming under pressure.

Major Jack Mathis stood beside him as Executive Officer, faithful as ever, uninterested in variety, committed to proximity. If Fred carried command, Mathis would carry weight as a twenty-five-year-old.

Major George "Axe" Axtell returned from Annapolis sharpened, not softened. By October he had assumed command of VMF-323, precision translated cleanly into authority. He ran the squadron exactly as he flew—ordered, intolerant of drift, with any errors corrected before they had time to multiply. Also, at twenty-three, he was seven months younger than Fred.

Major Hugh Russell took over VMF-313 at the ripe old age of twenty-six. Quiet. Competent. Men said things simply worked around him, which was its own form of leadership.

Major Quinton Johns joined him as XO, instinct paired with restraint, the two balancing one another without needing to explain it. Johns was one year younger than Russell, twenty-five.

Major Edmund Overend came back from China changed in ways he did not advertise. The Flying Tigers had taken their share of him, but he had given as much as he took. War compressed timelines. The Corps rewarded men who had already crossed a line and returned. Overend assumed command of VMF-321. He was twenty-nine.

Major Douglas Lenardson found his place— at age twenty-five, commanding Marine Photographic Squadron 354. His knowledge of technology, coupled with patience, qualified him for the position. Someone had to record what the rest would not have time to see, to provide intelligence and target data with truth rather than optimism.

Major Charlton Ivey took over a service squadron, which included logistics, sustainment, and the machinery that kept others alive long enough to matter. Not only was the job unglamorous, but also there was no margin for error. He was twenty-five years old.

Major Richard "Dick" Day was twenty-six when he returned stateside from Atlantic antisubmarine duty and took command of VMF-312. Day was steady and predictable, which was exactly what the moment required.

Major Gregory "Pappy" Boyington never stopped moving. At thirty-one, he was the "Old Man" of the brotherhood. He went from VMF-112 to take over VMF-214, hand-picked and lethal. He wore command the way he wore everything else—loosely, as if it were a jacket thrown over scars no one asked about.

They had all landed. Not together. Not cleanly. But alive, and useful.

Fred tried to keep track of the others. Letters went out. Replies came back when they could. Addresses changed. Call signs rotated. Names disappeared for weeks and returned with new titles and heavier margins. The war did not honor continuity. It rewarded usefulness. Some were thrown directly into engaged front line units. Others were assigned to units that were listed somewhere on a future operations planning board. Fred stopped trying to predict it.

At VMF-322, Fred and J.R. Mathis started with nothing and built forward. Aircraft were assigned. Pilots transferred in. Maintenance crews assembled from men who did not yet know each other's tells. The roster filled unevenly—some experienced, some barely out of training, all aware the work-up would be brief and the deployment would not. Wartime tours averaged fourteen months. Fred learned what command felt like on a scale.

Reputation hardened before he had time to examine it. Mathis handled gunnery the way he handled everything—without ceremony. Barrels warmed. Minds sharpened. Hesitation burned away. They drilled until mistakes became boring. They drilled until boredom became dangerous— and then drilled past it.

At night, when the line went quiet, Fred sometimes stood near the aircraft and listened to the metal tick as it cooled. He thought of all the "boys" who had landed elsewhere—well or otherwise—and of how narrow the margins still were, even with command stitched onto their collars.

The war was collecting them again.

Under different tail numbers. Under different commands. Under the same burning sky.

CHAPTER 26 – "YOU COMMAND, I CONTROL"

VMF-322 the "Cannon Balls" were built the hard way.

There was no ceremonial beginning, no day that could be pointed to as the moment the squadron arrived. There were only mornings that started earlier than planned, evenings that ended later than promised, and aircraft that demanded attention whether men were ready or not.

From July onward, Fred and J.R. Mathis lived on the flight line. Corsairs arrived in uneven numbers—airframes with hours already burned into their logbooks, replacements scavenged from wherever the Corps could spare them. Maintenance crews learned each plane's personality quickly. Some engines ran hot. Some landing gear remembered disrespect. Every aircraft carried a history, and none of them could be trusted until proven again. This aircraft was unforgiving. This aircraft was complex. This aircraft demanded focus. Accidents came quietly. A ground loop that bent a prop and shook confidence. A hard landing that cracked struts and bones alike. An engine stalling on approach. Some aircraft were written off. Some pilots were written off or walked off on their own.

Alone at the edge of the field one late evening, Fred was finishing a report when Mathis stopped beside him, hands in his pockets, looking out at nothing in particular.

"You ever notice," Mathis said, "how the quiet gets louder when you're done flying?"

Fred didn't look up. "Means you didn't bend anything important." Mathis nodded. Silence settled again.

"My younger brother washed out of flight training," Mathis said, almost casually.

Fred looked up. That was new.

"He wasn't a bad pilot," Mathis continued. "Just slow under pressure. Wanted it too much."

"What happened?"

Figure 13. Corsair cockpit controls.

"They offered him another billet. He took it. Flew a desk instead of a machine." Mathis shrugged. "He doesn't talk to me anymore."

Fred studied him. "You blame yourself?"

Mathis smiled thinly. "I taught him how I fly. Turns out that only works if you're wired the same way."

Fred set the clipboard aside. "What do you do with that?"

"You stop pushing people into shapes they don't fit," Mathis said. "You stop confusing courage with suitability." He looked back toward the darkened line.

"That's why I don't argue when you ground someone. Better embarrassed than buried."

The wind moved across the field.

"You ever wish you'd pushed him harder?" Fred asked.

Mathis shook his head. "No. I wish I'd noticed sooner."

After that night, Fred listened harder when decisions came down to margins—who flew again, who didn't. Trusting Mathis in those moments wasn't delegation. It was survival.

Fred did not believe in superstition. Luck maybe. Discipline definitely.

For that, he had Master Technical Sergeant Perry Dean Johnson.

#

The first time Fred met him, Johnson was standing on a step stool with his head inside a Corsair's wheel well, swearing softly at a leaking hydraulic line.

"Sir," Johnson said without looking out, "if you step one inch closer, this bird's going to kick you in the teeth." Fred stopped. Mathis grinned.

Johnson climbed down, wiped his hands on a rag older than half the squadron, and snapped a crisp salute— the kind that conveyed respect while implying he had better things to do.

"Master Technical Sergeant Perry Johnson. Been with the Corps since Hoover. If it flies, I can fix it. If it can't, I can bury it so far, the paperwork never finds you."

Mathis leaned in. "We keep this one."

From that day on, Johnson anchored the squadron. He kept the Corsairs alive, the crew chiefs running, and Fred and Mathis honest when ambition outpaced reality. No one outranked Johnson in common sense. No one tried.

Fred knew he had his senior enlisted after asking Johnson what he thought about building a unit from the ground up. Johnson didn't hesitate.

"Major, you command. I control. You make the decisions, the plans. I control the training, the resources, the people, and the hours in the day to make it happen. I'll keep you informed—and I'll keep you out of trouble." That was the deal.

From then on, Fred, Mathis, and Johnson functioned as one. Equipment lists. Personnel gaps. Facilities. Vehicles. Anything that matched the Table of Organization, they chased down. Anything they couldn't get, they worked around.

They trained close air support as if it were the only mission that mattered—because it was. Air superiority mattered. Interception mattered. But for Fred, the Marines on the ground would remember who showed up when they were pinned down. Communications were standardized. Radios tested, retested, and distrusted until proven again.

Brevity enforced until instinct replaced thought. Pilots learned to hear fear beneath clipped transmissions and translate it into ordnance delivered accurately and on time.

Mock villages. Tree lines. Ridge crests. Roads that became real enough to kill. Bombing patterns refined. Strafing passes measured in geometry and survivability, not bravado.

Mathis was relentless. Barrels glowed. Ammunition disappeared in disciplined arcs. Pilots learned to break off when instinct demanded one more pass—and to live because of it.

"Your job isn't to destroy," Mathis reminded them. "It's to come back and do it again tomorrow."

VMF-322 trained with the 1st Marine Division, then Army units—the 27th, the 96th—each with different habits and expectations. Fred insisted on integration, not accommodation. Fire support teams embedded. Ground officers learned who pilots were by their voices. Pilots learned terrain from descriptions spoken under stress. Sustainment followed. Fuel. Ammunition. Repair timelines. Runway patching under fire. Aircraft dispersion. Camouflage that worked. Pilots learned where their responsibility ended—and respected where someone else's began.

By autumn, VMF-322 was no longer learning how to train. The squadron was training as it would fight. On Oct 22nd, 1943, the squadron would have to ante up.

2 Oct 1943 – Range #38, Lt. Robert William Horn

Range #38 wasn't supposed to feel like a battlefield. It was scrub and sand, a strip of honest sky over ground that had no opinions. A place where the danger had rules. A place where the men still believed practice meant control.

The Corsair came in hard and loud, as always—engine full, airframe vibrating with the kind of power that felt like it could pull the world forward by force. The boys on the line watched it the way they watched everything new: with hunger, envy, calculation. Some of them were still learning to read an approach by posture and sound—high and clean, low and hungry, steady or chasing its own torque.

Horn was on that run.

Someone said his name. Not as a warning. As a point of pride. Horn had been coming along. He wasn't a legend. He wasn't a problem. He was one of them.

The aircraft dipped.

At first, it didn't look wrong, just a touch of wing, a correction. Then the correction happened again, too fast, like the airplane was arguing with the sky. The nose pitched, recovered, pitched again. The Corsair's sound changed. Not quieter—different. A note that made every head turn at once, instincts arriving before thought.

Someone shouted. The Corsair rolled.

Not a graceful bank. Not a disciplined turn. A snap—violent and ugly—one wing clawing higher as the other dropped like it had been punched. The airplane was still moving forward, still fast, but it was no longer flying the way pilots meant. It was flying the way gravity demanded.

Men started running before anyone shouted to run.

The Corsair hit the ground with a sound that didn't belong to training—metal taking the world personally, the air itself tearing. There was no clean explosion at first. The impact was a long, grinding violence, the kind that rearranged what was solid into fragments. A second later the fuel caught, and then the fire arrived: sudden, bright, hungry, too loud for something that had just been sky.

Someone screamed, "FIRE!" like the word could do anything.

Men rushed anyway. They piled into any vehicle available and rushed down range.

The crash trucks arrived late, wheels cutting ruts into sand. Hoses came alive and foam spat out in pale gushes that evaporated in heat. The fire fought them, shrinking, flaring, shrinking again, until it finally surrendered into smoke and twisted metal and the awful quiet that follows violence when the violence has decided it's done.

They ran with extinguishers that felt like toys against heat that had teeth. They ran with shovels, with bare hands, with nothing but the reflex to close distance on disaster because distance felt like cowardice. A chief grabbed an axe and went in, swinging into a shape that had stopped resembling an aircraft. The axe rang once—

high, useless—and the man recoiled as heat slapped him in the face.

"Horn! HORN!" Men kept shouting the name, as if volume could bring the living back out of flame.

The Corsair burned like it was offended. Like it had been forced into humiliation and meant to punish anyone close enough to witness it. Smoke poured downwind, black and oily, burning the throat before the eyes. The boys coughed, spat, wiped their faces with sleeves already dirty. They tried to get in again but couldn't.

Then—worse than fire—came the moment when everyone understood there was nothing left to do but watch it finish.

A pilot stood frozen with his helmet under his arm, mouth half open, eyes locked on the blaze. He looked like a man who'd just discovered the war had been waiting for him in peacetime. Someone behind him grabbed his shoulder and hauled him backward before he walked into it.

The men stayed there anyway.

No one spoke the next obvious question because everyone already knew the answer.

A crew chief finally said, hoarse, "Jesus."

A sergeant bent over, hands on knees, and vomited into the dirt like his body was trying to expel the sight.

Later—hours later—the Operations board would receive its first mark that mattered. Not a scribble. Not a note. A line. A name.

The hand that wrote it hesitated, then pressed harder, as if pressure could make it less real.

22 OCT 1943 – 2ndLt Robert William Horn – KIA – Range #38 – aircraft destroyed

When the chalk clicked against the board, the sound was too small. It was the first time the squadron learned that death could arrive with no enemy present and still take a man.

They would remember the fire. They would remember the smell. They would remember the way the Corsair's engine note had changed a heartbeat before it broke the world. After that day, every takeoff, gun run, landing carried a second meaning.

The words didn't land all at once. They arrived in pieces. Name first. Then the pause. Then the rest of it catching up.

Fred nodded because nodding was what men did when they understood something officially. Inside, nothing aligned. Horn wasn't supposed to be dead. Horn had been alive a few hours ago. He had been laughing that morning, helmet crooked, complaining about the heat like it was an inconvenience instead of a warning.

Fred realized, with a clarity that startled him, that this was the first man who had died while flying under his watch.

Not his fault. Not his decision. But his responsibility all the same.

That distinction would matter later. Right now, it didn't.

He walked alone to the edge of the field where the Corsairs sat cooling, their engines ticking softly as metal contracted. The airplanes looked unchanged. Identical. Innocent, even. Fred placed a hand against the fuselage of the nearest one—warm, solid, indifferent.

"This is what you do," he thought. Not angrily. Not accusingly. Just stating fact.

The Corsair didn't answer. It never would.

That night, Fred lay awake replaying everything that hadn't happened. The correction Horn might have made. The moment he might have pulled out. The fraction of a second where experience was supposed to save him and didn't.

Fred understood then that training accidents weren't accidents at all. They were previews.

Although the war hadn't started for him yet, it had introduced itself.

The next morning, Fred flew again. He strapped in, ran the checks, pushed the throttle forward. But something had shifted. He no longer flew to prove he belonged there. He flew to outlive the airplane long enough to bring others back.

He began watching pilots differently. Not for skill alone, but for hesitation. For overconfidence. For the way some men trusted the Corsair like a partner instead of a weapon that demanded obedience. Horn stayed with him after that. Not as guilt. But as gravity.

Every name that followed would stack on top of the first. But Horn was the one who taught Fred what command meant. You inherit authority when you take command. You also inherit responsibility for the walking dead. Once you do, you never give them back.

#

Training did not pause. It never did. Mathis took to gunnery like a man finally allowed to be honest. He ran the ranges until barrels glowed and ammunition belts emptied in clean arithmetic. Deflection shooting at speed. High angle passes that punished hesitation. He stood behind pilots at the firing line and spoke once, clearly.

"Commit," he said. "Or don't pull the trigger." No one argued. Physics enforced the lesson.

Maintenance learned the airplane alongside the pilots. The Double Wasp was reliable, but not patient. Torque punished sloppy throttle work. Tailwheel lock mattered. Landing gear remembered disrespect. Everything mattered. The line chiefs began to trust Fred— not because he was kind, but because he asked the right questions before something failed instead of after.

Evenings stretched long. Fred stayed late with squadron logs and weather charts, penciling routes and contingencies after the hangars went quiet. He carried Project George's lessons forward without naming them. Commitment points. Release decisions. Arrival without apology. Silence before consequence.

Fred tried to hone the mix of men, machines, and government into an effective squadron, without claiming ownership. He corrected when needed and trusted when earned. He learned when to press and when to step back. Sometimes the difference between failure and survival was not skill—but restraint.

By the end of December 1943, VMF-322 had lost a pilot and sustained 12 severely damaged or lost planes, due to take-off and landing accidents. The learning curve was steep.

Figure 14. Corsair during gunnery exercises.

CHAPTER 27 – MOVEMENT WEST

In late December, the orders arrived. VMF-322 and MAG-32 were headed west.

San Diego. There was no celebration.

Packing began immediately. Aircraft were prepped. Records closed. Men wrote quick letters, knowing the next chance would come later and harder. Fred gathered the squadron once.

"We're done practicing," he said. "Now we'll see what we remembered." No one asked where they were going after San Diego.

They already knew the answer lay across water.

VMF-322 had been forged in repetition, loss, and discipline. Whatever waited on the far side would not care how carefully they had prepared, only whether they arrived ready to answer.

#

January 1944. Movement orders never arrived dramatically. They came as administrative documents—typed, stamped, and routed through channels that treated distance like a math problem. Only the consequences carried weight.

VMF-322 left in pieces.

Aircraft went first. Corsairs lifted off in controlled intervals, climbing east before turning west, noses finally aligned with the war they had been preparing for. Ferry flights stretched across the continent, hopscotching from field to field, with the weather dictating pace and patience. Engines ran long. Tires developed flat spots overnight. Maintenance crews waited on unfamiliar ramps with tools already laid out.

The ground element followed by rail.

Troop trains pulled out before dawn, cars packed with seabags, flight gear, and men who had learned how to move without ceremony. Conversation rose briefly when the landscape changed, then fell away again as miles accumulated.

Enroute to San Diego, Early 1944

The train west moved like a living thing—jerking, shuddering, clattering across the continent with an entire squadron packed inside it. Johnson moved through the cars like a man who owned the railroad. "Sir," he reported to Mathis, "we're over our weight allotment by three thousand pounds."

Mathis didn't look up. "Solve it."

"I did."

"How?"

"By persuading an Army depot sergeant that he'd already issued us the extra crated parts. I didn't correct his memory. Would've been rude."

Fred shook his head. "Did you steal from the Army, Top?"

Johnson met his eyes, offended. "No, sir. I robbed them."

Johnson supervised loading, inventory, fuel drums, ammunition—down to where pilots slept. By the time the train crossed Mississippi, VMF-322 moved like a unit that had been together for years. Johnson made it so.

Winter slid past the windows—the Midwestern plains giving way to desert. Stops came at night. Meals were eaten quickly. Complaints were unnecessary.

Somewhere east of the Rockies, movement stopped feeling temporary. West became the only direction that mattered.

At stations along the way, men wrote letters they didn't finish and sealed them anyway.

\#

San Diego announced itself by smell—salt, fuel, kelp, steel.

The airfield lived at a tempo Cherry Point never had. Aircraft moved overhead day and night, various models layered together like a catalog of the war's ambition. VMF-322 reassembled gradually. Pilots arrived with new fatigue etched into posture. Maintenance unloaded crates carrying the squadron's history in spare parts and handwritten notes.

Aircraft logs were consolidated. Damage assessed. Airframes reassigned without sentiment.

Fred walked the flight line on the first morning, the Pacific flat and gray beyond the runways. This was not training airspace. Ships constantly moved offshore—transports, escorts, silhouettes sliding in and out of fog. Destinations were spoken here with future tense attached. Islands. Atolls. Objectives no one dated aloud.

Mathis joined him, hands in his jacket pockets. "Everything west of this," he said, nodding toward the water, "wants us yesterday."

Fred nodded. "We'll give them ready," he said. "That's all we can promise."

Routine resumed immediately. Test flights. Gunnery refreshers. Briefings rewritten for Pacific realities—range limits, ditching procedures, enemy aircraft profiles that still felt unreal on paper. The work sharpened, compressed by proximity. The men felt it.

San Diego wasn't an endpoint. It was a staging area—time folding inward and outward at once. Days passed quickly. Liberty was granted sparingly and taken without excess.

One evening, Fred stood at the edge of the field watching the last aircraft land against a darkening sky. He thought of how far they had come—and how irrelevant distance was about to become.

Movement west was complete.

What came next would not involve rails or schedules. Only arrival.

January–March 1944

San Diego became a holding pattern that refused to feel static.

From January through February 1944, VMF-322 trained as if the calendar itself were an adversary. Aircraft were refit with Pacific realities in mind—filters adjusted, corrosion hunted and neutralized, radios recalibrated for range rather than clarity. Engines were made to run harder and longer. Nothing was trusted, because nothing would forgive neglect once distance erased options. They flew daily.

Gunnery refreshers. Formation work. Navigation runs pushed farther offshore. Pilots learned how the Corsair behaved over open water—how light altered depth perception, how fatigue crept in when landmarks disappeared entirely. Maintenance was relentless.

Daily inspections became ritual. Salt found its way into everything. Control cables were checked and checked again. Ground crews learned to work faster without cutting corners, knowing the first mistake would not be the last one noticed.

The ground element trained as hard as the air crews. Enemy aircraft recognition filled classrooms— silhouettes burned into memory until Zeroes, Oscars, and Betty bombers required no thought. Captured weapons were passed hand to hand. Booby traps were explained clinically. Field sanitation lectures were taken seriously now; disease mattered almost as much as combat. Everyone cleaned something every day, aircraft, weapons, living spaces, habits. There would be no division between air and ground once they moved forward. They were all Marines, first and foremost.

Meanwhile, Fred searched for his brother Skid when he could. Records. Rosters. Movement lists passed quietly between desks. Submarine squadrons were the hardest to trace, their paths deliberately obscured. Skid's name did not appear anywhere Fred was allowed to look.

Silence did not mean loss. Loss did not always announce itself.

Fred held on to that.

\#

The news about Boyington arrived the same way.

Not as a briefing. Not as an announcement. It surfaced in fragments—an Operations note passed too quietly, a conversation that paused when someone else entered the room.

Mathis heard it first.

He was in the ready room cleaning a gunsight lens that didn't belong to him when the duty officer stopped in the doorway.

"Boyington" the man said. Nothing else.

Mathis looked up. "When?"

"January, around Rabaul, New Guinea. Shot down. Missing."

No confirmation. No recovery. No chute reported.

By the time Fred reached the hangar bay, Mathis was standing alone at the edge of the deck, helmet tucked under one arm, staring at the Pacific as if distance might explain something.

"They got him," Mathis said without turning.

Fred didn't ask who.

"Boyington," Mathis continued. " MIA."

The word missing settled differently than killed. Killed closed doors. Missing left them ajar, rattling in the wind.

"If anyone could make it down," Mathis added, "it'd be him." Fred nodded once. Probability, not hope.

The information spread without distortion. No one embellished it. No one joked. Boyington was not a legend to them. He was a reference point— someone who had defined margins each of the "Boys" were now expected to operate inside.

Lenardson read the notice twice and folded it carefully.

Axtell said nothing and returned to his charts.

Russell tightened tie-downs with more force than necessary and muttered something about distractions getting men killed.

Training did not pause. If anything, it sharpened.

Break-offs came sooner. Checklists were followed without shortcuts. Pilots flew cleaner, not bolder. Boyington's absence didn't inspire recklessness— it reinforced discipline. That, Fred realized, was the final lesson Boyington had left them.

Fred nodded once. That tracked. If anyone was there already, it would be Boyington.

They stood without speaking for a while. A Corsair was being secured nearby, chains rattling as deck crew worked with unhurried precision.

"Figures," Mathis said finally. "Guy never did believe in exits."

Later, in the ready room, someone asked the question that hovered around all of them.

"Think he made it down alive?"

Mathis didn't answer immediately. He took a sip of coffee that had gone cold, grimaced, and set the cup aside. "If anyone could," he said, "it'd be him."

That was not optimism. It was probability.

Fred thought of Boyington's voice—Don't let confidence turn into ego. They look identical from the outside. He recalled the way he flew at the edge not to tempt fate, but to define it.

He thought, too, of Skid. Of other men committed to environments that did not allow recovery. Of doctrines built around the acceptance that survival, sometimes, simply didn't report back on time. The next morning, training resumed exactly on schedule.

Engines turned. Deck cycles continued. Briefings proceeded without adjustment. The war did not pause for missing men, no matter how large they loomed in memory.

But something subtle changed. Somewhere ahead, the Pacific waited with the same indifference it always had.

Boyington is out there now. Either alive and beyond reach or gone beyond accounting.

Neither outcome altered what VMF-322 would do next.

The fight was still moving west.

If Boyington had taught them anything worth carrying forward, it was this: You didn't fly expecting rescue.

CHAPTER 28 – HAWAI'I

March 1944

In early March, movement orders came again—this time not across land, but across water.

Embarkation aboard the **USS Marcus Island**.

Figure 15. USS Marcus Island.

An escort carrier—small, purposeful, cramped. The flight deck looked narrow to men used to concrete margins.

From 7 to 13 March, VMF-322 lived aboard ship. Carrier operations came fast.

Takeoffs were short and committed. Landings demanded curved approaches, and discipline held to the last second. The Corsair remained unforgiving—its nose high, its landing gear honest only when treated correctly. Ensign Eliminator.

Fred watched with approval as young pilots learned to take the carrier deck cautiously.

Arresting wires snapped tight. Engines roared, then cut. Aircraft were cleared and re-spotted with practiced haste. The deck crew moved with choreography learned at cost. At sea, every man had a job beyond his specialty.

Pilots turned wrenches. Officers hauled stores. Everyone cleaned. Sweat and salt blurred distinctions. Maintenance was not delegated. It was shared.

Between sorties, briefings filled the hangar deck—enemy capabilities, likely responses, how Japanese air would meet them, and how quickly ground fire would follow.

The pilots listened differently now.

Less curiosity.

More subtraction.

Below deck, the air tasted of oil, sweat, and ocean.

Johnson stood with his clipboard, pen behind his ear, never still. Mathis joined him.

"Top, how's our readiness?"

Johnson flipped pages, scowled, shook his head, then looked up. "We'll be combat-capable the second the Navy stops treating my Corsairs like cargo. Engines were tied down wrong. Crates lashed like furniture. Sir, I'm convinced half the sailors on this ship think a carburetor is a French pastry."

Fred stepped closer. "Anything critical?"

Johnson hesitated a moment before answering: "We're good, sir. Better than good. I made a few acquisitions during loading."

Mathis sighed. "What did you take?"

"Nothing that anyone would miss and everything I could get my hands on to make us more lethal," Johnson said.

Fred didn't ask further.

At night, Fred stood at the rail and watched the water slide past—black, indifferent.

Somewhere out there—beneath layers of classification and steel—Skid lived by the same logic. Pressure instead of altitude. Silence instead of distance.

Somewhere closer, Pappy Boyington was either alive but beyond reach or gone beyond accounting. Neither possibility changed what VMF-322 would do next.

On the final day aboard Marcus Island, the squadron launched and recovered cleanly. No losses. No broken airplanes. No excuses recorded. That counted for something.

As Hawai'i came into range, the ocean softened its edge, blue returning where gray had ruled. The men leaned forward without saying why. Training was ending again. This time, the pattern did not suggest return.

Figure 16. Corsairs on flight deck.

CHAPTER 29 – MCAS EWA

Hawai'i rose gently, as if unwilling to startle anyone.

Green where the continent had been brown, humid where the air had been sharp with salt and fuel, the islands felt almost indecent in their calm. Palm trees bent in the breeze. Mountains held clouds in place like promises. It was difficult to reconcile the beauty with the inventory of ships crowding the harbor and aircraft circling overhead like persistent insects.

VMF-322 disembarked efficiently. No speeches. No ceremony. Just men stepping onto ground that already belonged to the war.

The tempo changed immediately fewer miles, more repetition. The Pacific was no longer a destination. It was a perimeter.

Their base settled into routine within days. Runways bordered by jungle. Hangars that never cooled. Aircraft that demanded attention whether flown or not. The Corsairs looked different here—less novel, more inevitable. They belonged.

Training resumed with a sharper edge, with live-fire exercises offshore, and close air support rehearsals over volcanic terrain that punished sloppy approaches and rewarded precision. Coordination drills with ground controllers continued until cadence replaced explanation. Radios became lifelines and liabilities—every transmission a decision made aloud, every hesitation recorded by someone listening. Operationally, VMF-322 was transferred from MAG-32 to the control of MAG-33.

The Maintenance crew ran without pause, fighting corrosion as salt crept into seams, connectors, habits. Engines kept running until they either failed or proved they wouldn't. Men learned what the airplane could survive—and what it would not tolerate twice.

Fred settled into command here.

The staff work multiplied—schedules, readiness reports, coordination meetings—but he refused to let the paperwork distance him. He walked the hangars daily, flew when it mattered, learned which pilots responded to pressure and which folded under it, and when silence corrected more effectively than words.

Mathis stayed exactly where Fred needed him.

Gunnery sharpened. Discipline stayed clean. When pilots cut corners, Mathis noticed. When they improved, he rewarded that too—less visibly. He ran the ranges until firing solutions became instinctive and breakoffs automatic.

"You don't win by staying," he told them. "You win by leaving alive."

Johnson ran the ground war. Crew chiefs rotated through aircraft like surgeons on a schedule dictated by wear and failure. Spare parts were tracked obsessively.

Anything that could be was pre-positioned, that is, stored away. Anything that couldn't was memorized. Johnson tolerated no superstition. "If you don't understand why it broke," he said, "it'll break again where you can't afford it."

Losses came, including a landing gear collapse that crushed confidence more than metal and a navigation error that ended in a long, quiet swim and a sober investigation. One pilot was grounded permanently— good hands, poor judgment under fatigue. Fred signed the papers himself and did not explain the decision beyond what was required. Hawai'i had lessons of her own still to deliver.

05 Apr 1944 –Hawai'i James F. Ingram/ Donald B. Houge

Hawai'i looked like safety from altitude. Green fields. White surf. A horizon that made promises. The kind of sky you could almost trust.

The Corsairs climbed clean, engines steady, sunlight glinting off wings like nothing bad could happen in a place that bright. Training flights moved with the disciplined boredom of men who had done the same thing so many times their bodies flew before their thoughts did. Ingram's aircraft was one of them—part of the pattern, part of the rhythm.

Then the rhythm failed.

It didn't fail dramatically. It failed with two lines converging, two minds making correct decisions in the same second that cancel each other out. An aircraft slid into the wrong place, or another drifted a fraction out of position, or the air itself shifted the way it always shifts, without asking permission.

Suddenly there were two Corsairs occupying one portion of the burning sky.

The collision wasn't a boom. It was a brutal crack—the sound of aluminum surrendering. The impact sent one aircraft yawing away, the other shuddering as if it had been struck by a giant hand.

For a heartbeat the Corsairs remained airborne, still committed to forward motion as if momentum could deny reality. Then a wing folded. Then a tail came apart. A pilot on a nearby wing keyed his mic and didn't speak— because there were no words fast enough to help.

Below, on the field, men looked up and watched two aircraft become wrong shapes.

One fell in a steep, fast arc that looked almost intentional until it wasn't, the pilot eventually gaining control back. The other corkscrewed, shedding fragments that glittered in the sun like confetti no one wanted.

Someone on the ground began counting under his breath. He didn't know he was doing it.

The aircraft hit beyond the line, far enough that the sound arrived late, and the smoke climbed in a slow column like it was reluctant to announce itself.

It took less than a minute for the truth to spread through the squadron, carried by voices that didn't need radios.

"Ingram's down."

Men ran toward the wreckage—of course they did. They ran even though they knew, even though the distance was too far and the burning sky had already decided. When they reached the site, the fire was smaller than Horn's had been. That made it worse. A contained blaze suggested there might be something inside worth saving.

The Corsair sat broken at an angle no engineer had ever designed, and the heat around it was a warning that did not need words. A crew chief stepped forward and stopped, jaw clenching as if he'd just bitten down on the fact of it. He turned away first. Not because he didn't care, but because caring didn't change anything.

They never saw each other. That was the part that stayed with Fred. They collided before anyone could speak. The formation was routine, spacing correct by regulation, the kind of drill flown often enough to dull the edge of caution. The sky over Ewa was clear, bright, deceptively generous. Corsairs climbed and turned through a practiced maneuver, engines steady, wings flashing in the sun.

Lt. James F. Ingram rolled first. Lt. Donald B. Houge followed.

The margin between them vanished in an instant.

Fred saw the geometry fail before he saw the impact—two aircraft converging into the same air space, timing off by less than a second, the Corsair's long nose hiding everything directly ahead until there was no room left to react.

The collision was brutal and final.

Metal struck metal at speed. One aircraft shattered immediately, breaking apart as if unzipped by force, debris flung outward in a widening arc. The second Corsair tore through the wreckage, wounded but still whole, staggering away trailing smoke and fragments of its own skin.

There was no radio call from Ingram. No parachute. His aircraft went down hard beyond the field, the impact sending a dark plume up from the cane that marked the end of the flight and the man inside it.

Houge's Corsair stayed airborne just long enough to make the damage undeniable. The aircraft was no longer flyable — controls compromised, structure failing—but Houge kept it level long enough to clear the field. He bailed out clean, chute snapping open against the blue, a single pale shape descending where moments before there had been two airplanes.

Fred stood rooted to the coral. One pilot fell under silk. One aircraft burning into the earth. The sky felt wrong—not hostile, not violent—just indifferent in a way Fred had not yet learned to accept.

Later, the paperwork would record it plainly:

05 APR 1944 Lt. Ingram—killed in mid-air collision. Aircraft destroyed

05 APR 1944 Lt. Houge—survived in mid-air collision. Aircraft destroyed

Clean lines. Accurate. Incomplete.

What the reports could not capture was the imbalance of it — how one man lived because his aircraft held together seconds longer, because altitude remained, because chance tilted slightly in his favor.

Fred watched Houge walk away hours later, shaken, silent, alive. That was when the loss truly landed.

Horn's death had been solitary—tragic, contained, distant. This was different. This was the first time Fred understood that survival did not mean safety, loss did not require recklessness or error—only proximity and timing. The Corsair, magnificent and lethal, did not forgive crowding or familiarity.

That night, Fred walked the flight line alone.

One empty revetment. One name crossed off the board.

One pilot breathing who would carry the moment forever.

The war had not begun yet. But the burning sky had already upped the ante.

From that day forward, Fred never again watched aircraft turn toward one another without counting seconds, angles, and distance—without remembering how little space separated life from death when men trusted the same piece of air.

Everything was incremental now. Errors narrowed. Margins tightened. Performance improved not through inspiration but through attrition of weakness.

They trained with infantry units rotating through the islands—men already burned by jungle and heat. Forward air controllers learned VMF-322's voices. Pilots learned how ground truth bent maps and how fear sounded when disguised as calm. Mock villages were built and destroyed repeatedly. Ridge lines memorized. Tree lines learned by shadow and sun angle.

The Corsair became second nature.

Pilots stopped fighting it and began commanding it. Takeoffs grew cleaner. Landings more disciplined. The airplane no longer felt hostile, just honest. It demanded respect every time and punished any lapse immediately.

Fred watched it happen without claiming credit.

He often thought of Project George. Of gliders committed without engines. Of the doctrine that said arrival mattered more than survival. Here, the doctrine had evolved. Survival enabled arrival. You lived so you could arrive again tomorrow, and the day after that, until the ground war ended or you did.

Fred's marriage wasn't destined to survive the long absences of the Glider assignment and his eventual move west to the Pacific. He received divorce papers during mail call one day, and with regrets he signed and returned them to Ellen.

CHAPTER 30 – C.W. "SKID" RAUSCHENBACH

March had folded into April. April into May. The war seemed to advance everywhere except where they stood, and that waiting carried its own pressure. Pilots rotated through leave reluctantly, sensing movement coming and not wanting to miss it. Fred continued to ask questions. Submarine schedules. Harbor movements. Names passed quietly between commands. One afternoon, a clerk hesitated when Fred asked again.

"Sir," the man said, lowering his voice, "you should check NAS Puunene, on Maui."

Fred filed a flight plan that day and headed over in the morning to do a fly-by.

Charles Wilmer "Skid" Rauschenbach, born in 1906, was Fred's older brother from a different mother. He was a half-brother. Charlie's mom died during his birth. His mother and Fred's father were both circus performers at the time. Aerial artists. She performed the "Iron Jaw" act.

In 1924, after recovering from a circus injury himself, Charlie, age 18, enlisted in the U.S. Navy, Submarine Force, as a deep sea and salvage diver. Fred was only 4 years old. So, Charlie was mostly a memory for Fred: the occasional story told over the passing time, a photo displayed on a shelf.

Charlie would have over 20 years of service in submarines, and 30 years total in the Navy. Starting as a Torpedoman, he graduated from diving school in 1933, with a record- setting dive at the time, of 325 feet under compressed air. He rose in enlisted rank to serve as Chief of the Boat on two submarines, USS30 (1937-1939) and USS NAUTILUS-SS 168 (1939-1940). In May 1939, while stationed on the east coast, he served as an instructor in using the Momsen Lung to rescue trapped sailors. He was also on the team that raised and salvaged the **USS SQUALUS** which sank while on sea trials off Portsmouth, NH.

He would retire as CWO-2.

Figure 17. "Skid" Rauschenbach in diving gear

In May 1939, while stationed on the east coast, he served as an instructor in using the Momsen Lung to rescue trapped sailors. He was also on the team that raised and salvaged the **USS SQUALUS** which sank while on sea trials off Portsmouth, NH. He would retire as CWO-2.

\#

The submarine was tied up, streaked with salt, crew moving quietly as if unwilling to disturb the dock with more noise than necessary. Fred buzzed the vessel, waving his wings as he screamed by at treetop level.

After landing, Fred stood at the bottom of the gangplank, scanning faces for one he had memorized from years earlier but had never expected to see again in this place.

Skid came down the gangway last.

Thinner. Older. Sunburned in a way that never entirely faded. He moved with the careful economy of someone accustomed to confined spaces and hard rules.

They stopped a few feet apart. Neither spoke first. Skid broke it with a crooked smile.

"Hell of a place to run into you."

Fred stepped forward and pulled him in hard, the sound of Skid's laugh muffled against his shoulder.

"I wasn't sure I'd get this chance" Fred said. "I've been searching for you since I joined up."

"Yeah," Skid replied. "That makes two of us."

It was a short visit squeezed between duty schedules neither of them could bend very far, with the unspoken thought that either or both of them, might not survive the war to meet again. They talked until the dock lights came on. They spoke about many things, but not about patrols. or losses. They talked around the war, acknowledging it without inventorying it. Shared meals followed. Skid looked at Fred's wings once, then away.

"You fly like you always did," he said. "Straight at the problem."

"You disappear into it," Fred answered. That seemed fair.

The reunion did not solve anything. It didn't need to. However, it proved survival still happens, even under rules designed to conceal it.

Figure 18. Skid Rauschenbach in dress blues.

Afterwards, in early September, Fred stood at the edge of the runway as Corsairs returned in sequence, engines howling, silhouettes sharp against the setting sun. Skid was scheduled to ship out again. This time on a surface ship, the **USS SPERRY,** which was a submarine tender. The island felt different now without him—less forgiving, more honest.

Figure 19. Skid Rauschenbach in Khakis.

The Pacific lay ahead, calm and deceptive. Training was ending. Whatever waited next would not allow rehearsal. This time, VMF-322 would not be arriving quietly.

Through summer, the island filled and emptied in cycles. Units arrived sharp and left sharper. News filtered in from forward areas, names, islands, casualty figures that felt abstract until they became familiar. VMF-322 trained with urgency disguised as routine. The whispers stopped being theoretical. Maps lingered longer on tables. Briefings grew shorter and more specific. The men stopped asking if and started asking when.

Fred watched the squadron he had built, move with quiet confidence now. Pilots spoke less and prepared more. Maintenance crews anticipated problems instead of reacting to them. Everyone understood their place.

By late summer, the squadron no longer talked about if they would deploy. They talked about where first. Rumors circulated. Names of islands spoken cautiously. Some pilots tried to guess based on ship movements. Others refused. Fred discouraged speculation. "You'll know when you need to," he said. "Until then, fly."

In September, the orders came. They were brief. Unsurprising. Final. VMF-322 was moving forward.

Fred gathered the squadron one last time beneath the hangar roof.

"We've done everything we can do here," he said. "What comes next won't care how prepared we feel. Only whether we act like it."

No one asked questions. By September of 1944, they were ready—not because they felt confident, but because nothing essential remained untested. The same was true for Fred's sister squadrons as well.
 The ante paid to the burning sky stood at:

VMF-312	6 Pilots Killed	18 Corsairs lost
VMF-322	2 Pilots Killed	16 Corsairs lost
VMF-323	3 Pilots Killed	20 Corsairs lost

As the aircraft were readied for movement and crates sealed once more, Fred stood alone near the runway, watching heat shimmer over concrete that would soon be behind them.

Hawai'i had not been a rest. It had been a testing ground. Testing his machines. Testing his men. Testing him. Now, the perimeter was about to move.

CHAPTER 31 – ESPIRITU SANTO

September 1944–March 1945

The Pacific closed behind them quietly.

VMF-322 departed Hawaiʻi in early September aboard **USS Breton,** the carrier already heavy with men who understood that each mile west stripped away another layer of abstraction. The island receded without ceremony. No bands. No speeches.

Just shoreline thinning until water took over entirely. The ship's rhythm imposed itself within days.

Figure 20. Cramped sleeping quarters on a hanger deck.

Sleep. Mess. Maintenance. Pre-Combat Checks. Gunnery Flights. Drills.

Briefings repeated often enough to become procedural rather than inspirational. Pilots spoke less. Ground crews inventoried more. The ocean was enough to absorb unnecessary conversation.

On 18 September 1944, **USS Breton** anchored off
Emirau in the St. Matthias Islands, New Guinea.

Figure 21. USS Breton (CVE-23).

The airfield felt temporary by intent, what with its
coral runways, revetments carved into vegetation, and
aircraft already wearing the residue of earlier operations.
This wasn't a place meant to be used but not improved.
VMF-322 disembarked quickly, unloaded efficiently, and
confirmed what they already suspected.

They stayed just long enough to exhale and move
again.

On 1 October, orders sent them south to Espiritu
Santo, New Hebrides. On 25 October, Fred and several
pilots moved ahead, hopping through staging points
without lingering. Guadalcanal appeared briefly beneath
their wings—the name still heavy with ghosts. Burned-out
hulks sat close enough to active runways to remind them
how recently survival there had been uncertain.

134

From there, they continued to Espiritu Santo.

If Emirau had felt temporary, Espiritu Santo felt crowded with intention.

Espiritu Santo – Late 1944 - 1945

Humidity wrapped around them like wet canvas. The air smelled of rot, fuel, and effort already spent by others who had arrived earlier and left nothing behind but scars on the ground.

Johnson stepped off the transport before the officers even unbuckled.

"Listen up!" he barked at the enlisted Marines behind him. "We are not waiting for the Navy to unpack our gear. We find ground. We claim it. We build it." By the time Fred and Mathis reached the designated bivouac area, Johnson had already:

- Defined a perimeter.

- Assigned work crews.

- Marked drainage trenches.

- Claimed a strip of hard dirt near the operations hut.

- Convinced a Seabee chief to loan him a bulldozer "for an hour," which meant permanently.

Fred watched tents rise, crates get lashed, and Marines move with purpose sharpened by familiarity.

"How long's he been doing this?" Fred muttered.

Mathis smirked. "Since the Spanish American War, maybe."

Johnson turned and shouted, "Sir! Welcome to your new kingdom. Give me a day and it'll look like a place fit for Marines."

It wasn't, but it would be—because Johnson willed it so.

Espiritu Santo was not glamorous. It was infrastructure war—aircraft maintenance, fuel distribution, logistics, disease control, and weather management layered over jungle that resisted all of it.

The rain came hard and without apology.

Runways softened. Revetments slumped. Mosquitoes arrived in clouds thick enough to be audible. Men learned quickly that discipline extended beyond aircraft and weapons. Boots were dried. Feet inspected. Cuts cleaned aggressively. Malaria briefings were enforced without exception.

\#

VMF-322 flew daily.

Not into combat yet—but close enough to feel the edges of it. Navigation legs stretched longer. Fuel margins tightened. Radio discipline became mandatory rather than recommended. Pilots learned to identify friendly ships by silhouette alone and enemy aircraft by instinct.

They trained with purpose now, not anticipation.

Fred ran the squadron hard without spectacle. Schedules were published and kept. Expectations were clear and non-negotiable. Pilots rotated through missions designed to exhaust them slightly beyond comfort. Ground crews worked until sweat and rain erased the difference.

Losses arrived indirectly. Landings. Take-offs. Engine failure. Replacement pilot inexperience. VMF-322 lost three more planes flying out of Luganville Airfield to landing or take-off incidents. Aircraft were diverted due to weather and never seen again. Pilots were reassigned forward and not replaced. Rumors from other units filtered in—bad landings, bad luck, bad timing. Espiritu Santo absorbed them all without comment.

By December, the tone shifted again. Maps stayed open longer. Names appeared in briefings that had not been there before. Okinawa surfaced once, then again. Luzon. Iwo Jima. The geometry of the war was narrowing.

Fred stood more often at the edge of the strip, watching aircraft launch into air that refused predictability. He thought of Hawai'i as a proving ground. Espiritu Santo was something else. A funnel.

VMF-322 was no longer training to deploy. They were waiting for the order to move into it. When the word finally came—quietly, without ceremony—it carried no surprise. They would be heading north. They would be flying close air support. They would be flying it daily.

Fred gathered the squadron once, briefly.

"We're not going somewhere new," he said. "We're going somewhere familiar that just happens to be trying to kill us." No one laughed.

Outside, Corsairs sat in revetments carved into red earth, engines ticking as they cooled, paint already dulled by climate and use.

Espiritu Santo had done its work. It had taken a squadron and turned it into a machine that could endure. The next place would decide what that endurance cost.

CHAPTER 32 – ELAINE

Elaine McClayton did not leave because she had to.

Baltimore gave her every reason to stay. The McClayton house stood back from the street, solid and self-possessed, the kind of place where voices rarely rose and decisions were made privately before being presented as inevitable. Her father, William McClayton, moved through those rooms with the practiced ease of a man long accustomed to public life. Maryland politics had shaped him, its patience, its choreography, its belief that appearances were never accidental.

Elaine understood that world. She had learned early how to listen without revealing, how to speak carefully without diminishing meaning. She accompanied her father to events without resentment, stood where she was placed, and smiled when expected. By 1942, when William McClayton decided his name could carry him to Congress, Elaine knew the routines by heart: the dinners, the conversations that circled without answering, the quiet faith that order itself could keep uncertainty at bay.

Her marriage, which began in 1941, fit neatly into that life. Her husband wore an Army officer's uniform and believed in structure, progress, and the satisfaction of doing what was required. When he shipped to Europe, the marriage changed without declaration. Letters replaced presence. Updates replaced intimacy. His words were competent and careful, written by a man advancing by coordinates and orders rather than by emotional distance.

Elaine read each letter thoroughly. She never criticized him. She never complained.

She simply became aware of a truth she had not expected: duty could exist without closeness, and vows did not prevent solitude.

\#

When the Red Cross passed through Baltimore seeking women for overseas field service, Elaine listened differently than she once would have. Not with urgency. Not with fear. With recognition. The work was not decorative. It was logistical, exhausting, and intimate in ways politics was not. It required competence rather than performance—usefulness rather than approval.

Her father regarded the idea calmly.

"This will reflect well," he said. "Temporary service. Appropriate."

Elaine nodded, understanding the words without accepting their meaning.

She trained quickly and without complaint, discovering she was good at the work. She absorbed protocols, procedures, and the discipline of helping without promising outcomes. When her father's campaign ended unsuccessfully later that year, it barely registered. She was already elsewhere in her mind.

The Pacific orders came quietly. "It's a long way," her father said. "Yes," Elaine replied. "That's why I asked for it."

Her husband's response arrived weeks later. He did not forbid her. He did not praise her. He reminded her—politely—that she was still married. Elaine folded the letter and placed it with the others. The marriage had not ended. But it had stopped moving forward, suspended by distance and a silence she did not know how to address.

Espiritu Santo bore no resemblance to Baltimore. There were no structures built to impress, no rules designed to reassure. Men arrived already exhausted or soon became so. The work never announced itself as important; it simply was.

Figure 22. Elaine McClayton/MacMillan Red Cross.

Elaine learned how to listen without intruding, how to offer comfort without implying resolution. She learned when mail mattered and when it did not. She learned to recognize the men who needed to speak and those who needed quiet.

She adjusted to the rhythms of the base until they no longer felt foreign. She did not expect to meet anyone.

\#

They encountered each other by accident. Elaine was standing near a makeshift canteen, reconciling inventories that never quite aligned with reality, when a man slowed nearby, watching with the detached attentiveness of someone already carrying too much responsibility.

"You're not from here," he said.

"Neither are you," she replied.

He smiled faintly. "Baltimore?"

Elaine paused. "Yes."

"Born there," he said. "Feels like another life now." That was enough.

They spoke first of the city—streets, weather, the harbor's particular smell in summer. Rank followed later, exchanged carefully. Names were exchanged after that. There was no urgency to explain themselves. He did not linger longer than necessary. When he left, she watched him go without turning.

Elaine returned to her work, knowing without surprise that the moment would not remain isolated. Espiritu Santo had already taught her this: some meetings did not announce themselves. They took root quietly.

Figure 23. Elaine with local natives.

Fred did not think about her again until that evening. The day had been ordinary in the way wartime days were—maintenance issues, one aircraft refusing reliability, a pilot pushing past fatigue Fred could see before the man admitted it. The work left no space for distraction. Only later, walking the perimeter road as the air cooled enough to breathe, did the conversation return uninvited. Baltimore. The way she had spoken it without nostalgia or apology.

In wartime, anything that insisted on being remembered usually mattered.

Over the following days, they crossed paths again, without making arrangement, near the infirmary, by the letter station, walking the same dust-choked road at dusk. They spoke honestly but selectively, neither crossing lines that did not need naming.

Elaine did not mention her father's politics. Fred did not speak of his divorce.

Eventually, she said, "I'm married."

"I know," he replied.

"I don't know what this is."

"I don't either."

They left it there. They made no promises. They did nothing reckless.

They fell in love anyway—slowly, carefully, in spaces defined as much by restraint as by presence. In a war that consumed certainty, their connection remained unresolved, unfinished, and therefore real.

\#

For the months leading up to March 1945, VMF-322 lived in pre-combat operations. Nothing about it felt like waiting. They flew daily. Navigation runs punished imprecision. Gunnery exercises offshore corrected missed angles without sentiment. Close air support rehearsals were refined until timing to ground units was measured in seconds.

Elaine and Fred would find each other again and often, without forcing it.

Enemy contact remained distant but persistent. Reconnaissance reports filtered in. Japanese aircraft probed at the edges of range without committing. Fred demanded restraint without hesitation. No chasing ghosts. No wasted sorties. No heroics that did not return with value.

Maintenance became survival. Humidity punished metal relentlessly. Cannibalization occurred without debate. Aircraft were grounded early to avoid being lost late. Loss arrived anyway.

She stepped outside late one evening to let the heat bleed off her shoulders. Fred sat nearby on a crate, jacket off, sleeves rolled, studying a clipboard he was not reading.

"You keep strange hours," she said.

"Seems inefficient to waste daylight." She leaned against the crate opposite him.

"I almost asked for a transfer," she said.

"Why didn't you?"

"I wasn't sure what problem I was trying to solve."

"Okinawa," Fred said eventually.

She understood what it carried. "You'll go."

"Yes."

"When?"

"Soon enough."

They did not touch. They did not need to.

By February 1945, briefings lengthened. Maps stopped being generalized. Okinawa appeared and stayed. Pre-combat operations ended not with an announcement, but with the realization that the next sortie would not be rehearsal.

Elaine walked with Fred as far as the junction one night.

"I won't ask you to write," she said. "And I won't pretend I don't want you to."

"I won't make promises I can't keep."

"That's why I trust you."

She handed him a small, folded slip of paper.

"In case," she said. "Only if." Fred took it carefully.

"Be careful," he said.

"You too."

She turned first.

Fred watched until the dark reclaimed its share, then stood another moment to let the direction settle inside him. The road pulled him back toward the squadron. The war waited without comment. What he carried from Espiritu Santo was not a promise. Not a regret.

It was something quieter—and more dangerous. Something worth surviving for.

Elaine—POV

(Espiritu Santo, Late 1944 to Early 1945)

Elaine learned quickly that war did not announce itself the way civilians expected.

There were no crescendos. No single moments that declared this matters. Instead, importance accumulated quietly—through repetition, through exhaustion, through the way men stopped asking questions once answers no longer helped.

Her days began early. Inventory sheets never matched reality, so she learned to trust patterns instead of numbers. Bandages disappeared faster than anticipated. Morphine required discretion. Letters arrived in bunches and left individually. She learned who needed their mail immediately and who needed it delayed by a day, sometimes two, until they could read without breaking.

Espiritu Santo did not reward sentimentality. It tolerated competence. Elaine became competent. She learned the language of men who did not want reassurance. She learned how to listen without filling silence. She learned how to recognize the moment when a joke was a request for grounding, and when quiet was a form of prayer.

Her marriage occupied a different space now—not painful or urgent, but simply inert. Letters still arrived from Europe, methodical and intact. Her husband wrote as if time were something to be measured and survived rather than inhabited. Elaine answered with care and brevity. She did not lie. She did not confess. The distance required neither. She told herself this was stability.

The man she noticed did not arrive with drama. He was already there moving through the base with the unremarkable confidence of someone whose authority did not need reinforcement. He did not look at her the way men often did. He did not scan for opportunity or relief. When he spoke, it was because he had decided speech was efficient. That, more than anything, unsettled her.

They spoke first about Baltimore. Not nostalgically. Precisely. Streets. Weather. The smell of the harbor in summer. Shared geography, stripped of obligation. It was the safest possible intimacy.

She noticed how carefully he kept his boundaries. How he ended conversations before they drifted. How he never asked questions that required explanation. She recognized discipline when she saw it. She had grown up around it—political, social, marital. This was different.

This was operational.

Elaine did not tell him about her father. She did not tell him about the campaign, or the house, or the life she had stepped away from. He did not tell her about his divorce. They both understood that disclosure created gravity—and gravity was already working against them. What developed did not feel reckless. That was the danger.

They met where routines overlapped: near the infirmary, at the edge of the supply depot, on the same stretch of road at dusk where heat finally loosened its grip. They never planned it. They never named it. The war provided enough structure to make coincidence plausible.

Elaine remained married. He remained committed elsewhere. Neither pretended otherwise.

"I don't know what this is," she said once.

"I don't either," he replied.

That honesty felt rarer than certainty.

She watched him work.

Not closely—she was careful about that—but attentively enough to understand the shape of him. He carried responsibility the way some men carried rank: without flourish, without complaint, and without allowing it to excuse error. When pilots returned shaken, he noticed before anyone else did. When maintenance crews needed time, he gave it without calling it mercy.

He did not posture. He absorbed.

Elaine understood why men followed him. It was not charisma. It was containment.

She also understood the cost. When he said "Okinawa," he did not say it like a destination. He said it like an equation already solved.

She did not ask him to stay.

She did not ask him to write.

She did not ask him to promise.

Elaine had learned that asking the wrong question was sometimes worse than silence.

What they shared existed entirely within restraint. They did not cross lines because neither of them needed to test what would happen if they did. The knowledge was enough. Presence was enough.

That was how she knew it mattered.

As the months passed, the base changed texture. Briefings lengthened. Maps lost abstraction. Names stopped rotating off lists. Elaine noticed the way men packed differently. Not hurried—deliberate. She noticed which jokes disappeared first.

She watched Fred recede—not emotionally, but operationally. Command did not harden him. It consumed space. She did not resent that. She respected it.

The night they parted, there was nothing cinematic about it.

No rain. No music. No final words that pretended to solve anything.

"I won't ask you to write," she said. "And I won't pretend I don't want you to."

"I won't make promises I can't keep."

"That's why I trust you."

She gave him a piece of paper—not an address exactly, not a plan. Just a way back if.

Elaine understood something then with absolute clarity:

This was not love that demanded survival.

This was love that made survival meaningful.

She returned to her quarters alone and did not cry. She folded herself back into routine. Patients still arrived. Supplies still vanished. Men still needed listening more than reassurance. The war did not pause for clarity. Elaine continued doing what she had learned to do best, present without illusion, useful without expectation, steady without pretending permanence.

Somewhere beyond the island, aircraft lifted and vanished into distance. She did not imagine him in them. She did not need to. What mattered was not the outcome.

It was that, for once in her life, she had chosen something without needing it to be sanctioned, explained, or justified. That knowledge stayed with her. Quietly.

CHAPTER 33 – SECRET DESTINATION

On 2 March 1945, he lifted off at first light and headed est toward the Admiralty Islands. Fred left Espiritu Santo alone for briefings at higher HQ. The flight was long enough to empty thought of everything but fuel, instruments, and horizon. Sea replaced land quickly. The radio stayed disciplined and spare. No calls mattered beyond position checks and weather.

He landed at Pityilu Island with dust still settling behind the tires, shut down, and climbed out without ceremony. The field was busy in the way forward places always were, with aircraft arriving, aircraft leaving, nothing lingering long enough to deserve familiarity.

The wait stretched.

Briefings came without substance. Schedules shifted without explanation. Names appeared on boards and disappeared again before anyone could ask why. Fred slept lightly and walked often, learning the contours of a place that would never know his name.

He returned to Espiritu Santo with information and intelligence he could not yet share.

On 26 March, the call finally came. Transport by carrier. The harbor smelled of fuel and anticipation. Ships rode low and ready; decks already stained with use.

From 27 to 31 March, White Plains moved west under a discipline that discouraged curiosity. The ship's routine asserted itself immediately—flight operations at dawn, maintenance all day, briefings without destinations, charts kept covered.

Fred and VMF-322 boarded **USS White Plains (CVE-66)** with a small bag and a larger understanding: whatever came next could still not be briefed.

Figure 24. USS White Plains (CVE-66).

Aircraft were sighted, lost from view, and sighted again. Pilots flew deck cycles that existed purely to keep edge sharp. Engines were run and shut down. Guns were cleaned. Ammunition was issued.

During a pre-deployment check, an enlisted Marine asked a procedural question one level above his pay grade. Fred answered automatically.

"If I go down, Mathis will sort it." The Marine nodded, reassured.

Mathis, hearing it from across the tent, said nothing.

Later, when Fred walked past him, Mathis gave the smallest shake of his head—don't say that out loud—and Fred allowed himself a rare, quiet smile. The line would mean nothing until the day it meant everything.

Below decks, rumors failed to gain traction. The men stopped guessing.

At night, Fred stood on the catwalk and watched the wake stretch out behind the ship, white against black water—a path that could not be followed back. The Pacific felt different now—no longer wide, no longer abstract, but compressed by silence into something immediate.

31 Mar 1945 1930Z

On the morning of the 31st, the sea changed color. That was the only warning. Green shifted to gray. The air carried something metallic. The ship altered course slightly—a correction small enough to look accidental and purposeful enough to matter.

Fred leaned over the rail as the sky burned down from orange to red to purple. The sea ceased to be water.

It became scale.

More than a thousand ships lay framed in silhouettes.

USS White Plains carried sixty-four F4U-1D Corsairs on deck—those of VMF322 and Major George "Ax" Axtell's VMF-323. Nearby, **USS Hollandia** held the thirty-two Corsairs of VMF-312, under Major Richard "Dick" Day.

Fred felt it settle then—the way weight redistributes once momentum commits.

Once briefed, the squadron moved differently. Less talk. More preparation. The kind of mission focus that doesn't require instruction because it has already learned what comes next. Training had ended months ago.

Now there was only arrival—timed, deliberate, unrecoverable. Whatever shore lay ahead would reveal its secrets before long.

CHAPTER 34 – OPERATION ICEBERG

Fred saw it as density first. Steel layered upon steel, wakes overlapping until the surface looked stitched together by motion. Ships filled the horizon in every direction, rising and falling with the swell, silhouettes stacked so tightly it felt as if the Pacific itself had been requisitioned for service. This was not a fleet.

Figure 25. US 5ᵗʰ Fleet/TF-58.

Over 1,400 U.S. and Allied vessels, 3,000 aircraft, and over 180,000 soldiers and Marines in the initial attack. Battleships lay broadside and immobile, guns already elevated, barrels the length of freight cars. Cruisers slid between them like attendants. Destroyers paced farther out, hunting threats that had not yet announced themselves. Transports crowded the inner

151

lanes, decks packed with men and vehicles, ramps ready, boats already swinging outward.

Above it all, aircraft circled—fighters high and watchful, bombers assembling in disciplined geometry, spotting planes already correcting fall of shot. Escort carriers rode low, compact and busy, flight decks crowded with Corsairs spotted wingtip to wingtip.

VMF squadrons 322 and 323—waited aboard USS White Plains.

VMF-312 was loaded on USS Hollandia, engines warm, pilots strapped in. Fred stood on the catwalk and counted without knowing why.

Figure 26. USS Hollandia (CVE-97).

Everywhere he looked there was movement with purpose. Nothing drifted. Nothing hesitated. It was the largest force he had ever imagined—more ships than in Normandy, more steel than the war had yet demanded in one place. Somewhere ahead lay Okinawa. Somewhere behind him lay thousands of miles of ocean, and every harbor was already emptied to make this possible.

Fred knew the plan well enough to recite it. What he didn't know—what no one knew—was how it would survive first contact. The Japanese did not contest the beaches. That alone should have felt wrong.

The U.S. forces for the Battle of Okinawa (Operation Iceberg) were organized under the Tenth United States Army, a joint-service command led by Lieutenant General Simon Bolivar Buckner Jr.

The Tenth Army had two combat corps, one made up of Army Divisions, and one made up of USMC Divisions along with multiple support and logistical units:

XXIV Corps (U.S. Army) 7th, 27th, 77th, and 96th Infantry Divisions

III Amphibious Corps (USMC) 1st, 2nd, and 6th Marine Divisions

The invasion was supported by the largest naval armada of the Pacific War, consisting of over 1,500 ships, including allied ships from Canada, UK, New Zealand, and Australia.

Tactical Air Force, Tenth Army: A joint Army-Marine Air Force command belonged to the Tenth Army, providing dedicated air support. Because of the very large number of kamikaze threats, the Air Defense Command was a critical early unit to go ashore. Utilizing the day and night fighters' squadrons from three different Marine Aircraft Groups. This command group would be responsible for assigning all defensive and offensive sorties.

Nearly sixty thousand men would step onto Okinawa that morning. Before it was over, three times that number would pass through the island.

Naval gunfire rolled inland in measured salvos, ridgelines collapsing into smoke. Return fire was minimal. Observation aircraft reported nothing moving. Gun flashes were scarce. No massed infantry. No desperate counterattacks.

It looked easy. Fred knew better. The enemy on Okinawa was not forward. They were buried.

Figure 27. LTG Simon B. Buckner.

#

Lieutenant General Mitsuru Ushijima had chosen defensive depth over opposing the beach landings. Allowing the landings, preserving strength inland where caves and tunnels linked firing positions into something that could absorb punishment indefinitely. Reverse slopes. Interlocking sectors. Entire regiments living underground, waiting not to repel the invasion, but to pin it down and then grind it up.

Figure 28. LTG Mitsuru Ushijima.

The Japanese defense of Okinawa was the final and bloodiest major engagement of the Pacific War, lasting from April 1 to June 22, 1945. Lieutenant General Mitsuru

Ushijima led the Japanese 32nd Army hoping to force a negotiated peace rather than an unconditional surrender.

The 32nd Army had approximately 100,000–110,000 personnel, including regular army units like the 24th and 62nd Divisions, 9,000 Imperial Japanese Navy troops, and nearly 40,000 conscripted Okinawan civilians.

The Shuri Line: The core defensive network centered around Shuri Castle, utilizing a series of concentric ridges (such as Hacksaw Ridge and Kakazu Ridge) to create overlapping fields of fire.

01 April 1945, the first waves crossed Hagushi beaches under a burning sky filled with smoke from naval guns. Men stepped off ramps expecting machine-gun fire—and found only surf, wind, and ground that had not yet decided to answer.

By noon, thousands were ashore. Both Yontan and Kadena Airfields were secured relatively unopposed on 01 April.

Figure 29. Okinawa beach head

By nightfall, they were uneasy. III Amphibious Corps pushed north unopposed. Villages stood intact. Roads lay open. Fields were undisturbed. Everything looked usable. Nothing looked.

To the south, XXIV Corps advanced cautiously. Engineers cleared roads. Patrols returned with nothing to report but silence. Then artillery began to appear—not massed, not persistent, just enough to mark direction. Mortars fired once and vanished. Machine-gun nests delayed movement, then disappeared underground. Japanese forces withdrew south, trading ground for time. They were building something inland.

02 Apr 1945

The Assault Element of VMF(N)-543 aboard the **USS ACKERNER** (AKA-53) at anchor was attacked after midnight by a Sonya kamikaze. Five men were injured and two vehicles were destroyed. It was a sign of what tomorrow held for Fred and VMF-322.

03 Apr 1945

The predawn message reached Fred without ceremony, while onboard the USS WHITE PLAINS:

LST-599. Hit at dawn. Kamikaze attack. Burning. Cargo destroyed.

He did not need to read the rest to know that his plan had not survived first enemy contact.

Figure 30. LST-599 After kamikaze attack.

Fred knew exactly what that ship carried because he had signed for it all— every crate, every pallet, every barrel and biscuit that would make VMF-322 functional He read the dispatch once. Then again. Stripped it down to survivable facts.

The men were alive. That mattered most. One Officer, six enlisted injured, of which two required evacuations to a hospital ship.

Everything else—the ground echelon, vehicles, fuel, tools, spare parts—had gone into the fire or the sea. What flames had not taken, saltwater had finished. The margin beneath the airplanes was gone before they ever touched land.

VMF-322 was no longer whole.

One part remained at sea aboard White Plains— aircraft intact, pilots ready, waiting for a runway that could be trusted. Another part lay offshore near Kadena, on sister LST-598, living out of seabags and borrowed canvas, trying to turn coral and mud into an air station. The rest—what made a squadron sustainable—was nowhere in the theater yet.

Fred folded the message.

Okinawa did not pause for logistics.

He moved toward the MAG-33 operations cell, finding it already alive with radio traffic and map boards. What followed was not a meeting so much as alignment. Fred did not ask for anything that did not exist. He asked what could be spared without breaking someone else first.

Fuel could be rationed differently. Tools duplicated. Crews overlapped. Vehicles pooled and argued over later. Nothing was promised. Nothing was written down.

By the afternoon of April 3rd, Fred accepted what could not be changed. VMF-322 would land light, and it would stay that way for days, if not weeks.

The squadron would fly because it had to.

CHAPTER 35 – GROUNDED

Days passed.

Task Force combat air patrols circled continuously overhead, fighters trading altitude and fuel for vigilance. Carriers held position offshore, decks crowded, engines cycling, their presence both stabilizing and insufficient. On land, engineers and Seabee's worked coral and mud into something that might eventually support flight—if time allowed and enemy fire did not interrupt the attempt.

What remained of VMF-322's squadron ground echelon reached Kadena, on 6 April. They arrived without the equipment meant to make arrival meaningful. No vehicles. No fuel trucks. No proper maintenance shelters. They carved order out of shortage, laying out bivouac areas with borrowed tools, marking spaces that would one day hold aircraft. The sound of engines passed above them daily—close enough to measure by pitch, distant enough to remain unreachable.

The supply element never arrived. Not then. Not when expected.

It remained somewhere behind the war, tied up in anchorages and schedules that mattered to someone else. The men marked the absence quietly and worked around it. They had already learned that shortages did not announce themselves as emergencies. They simply shaped what was possible.

Fred noted the gap once and moved on.

\#

By the time USS White Plains finally turned back toward Okinawa on 9 April, VMF-322 existed in three disconnected pieces—aircraft at sea, ground crews ashore, and supply stretched between them—linked only by radio calls and intent. The airplanes would bring them together. What lay beneath them would have to be invented. The invasion did not pause. It never did.

Between April 3rd and 9th, Fred sat through briefings that no longer attempted reassurance. Reality settled in. The Japanese were not contesting ground. They were shaping it. Every road became a funnel. Every ridge masked something. Entire companies advanced without seeing an enemy until suddenly they were pinned from three directions by fire that seemed to come from the rock itself.

Lieutenant General Mitsuru Ushijima and the Shuri Line announced their presence with precision fires, not as a wall, but as defense in depth that could not be bypassed. Artillery observers began calling for sustained fire. Naval guns resumed their work farther inland, flattening visible positions that were already empty. Infantry units advanced into ground that looked devastated and found fresh fire waiting anyway. The land absorbed punishment and returned it selectively, with patience.

On the beaches, replacement units continued to arrive. The scale grew daily—men, machines, ammunition, fuel. Okinawa became crowded with intention.

Still, the airfields remained unused.

#

Kadena and Yontan were occupied quickly, but occupation did not equal control. Engineers moved in immediately, filling craters, marking hazards, clearing debris. Japanese artillery ranged the fields sporadically— shells arriving without pattern but with accuracy, zeroed just enough to force pauses in work and remind everyone that visibility did not mean safety. The airfields were prizes—but not yet assets.

04 Apr 1945

MAG-33 headquarters element and advance party arrived at Kadena to coordinate construction, air defense, and flight operations ahead of the group squadrons. They worked under fire they could neither fully predict nor immediately suppress.

06 Apr 1945

Japanese air attacks intensified offshore. Radar picket ships took the first hits. The burning sky was filled with defensive CAPs, fighters vectored hard to intercept threats that no longer pretended they intended to survive. Kamikazes came in calculated streams, routes chosen to saturate defenses.

From the carriers, Marine pilots watched columns of smoke rise from ships they had departed days earlier. They stayed aboard because they had to.

On land, infantry learned the rhythm of Okinawa—advance, stop, dig, absorb fire, advance again. Casualties accumulated not in dramatic surges but in steady subtraction.

Ground assault echelons from VMF-312, VMF-322, and VMF-323 arrived and linked up with the MAG-33 advance party, unloading what little they had and claiming ground that would soon need to support more than tents and radios.

\#

At 1530Z, **Colonel Raymond C. Scollin**, USMC—Air Base Commander of Kadena—was wounded and evacuated. He had been in the control tower across from the dump, performing his duties, when struck in the head by a 20-millimeter round. Leadership was becoming a valuable commodity already. Unloading continues.

Alerts sounded at **1850hr and 2035hr.**

07 Apr 1945

It was clear the battle would not resolve quickly. The northern end of the island was secured. The beaches were firm. Supply flowed. But the south held—anchored by caves and ridges that refused reduction by bombardment alone. All squadrons were engaged in the unloading and establishing of bivouac sites. Enemy strafed the airfield twice, causing ammunition dump to explode.

Okinawa was not stalling. It was settling in.

There were three alerts at **0330**, **1405**, and **1820**.

CHAPTER 36 — ANGELS OF OKINAWA

09 Apr 1945

It was at Okinawa the Corsair was given the nickname "Angels of Okinawa" due to their success against Japanese aircraft.

The call finally came. The airfields were ready enough. The situation demanded more air power than carriers alone could sustain. Marine Aviation Group 33 (MAG-33) would move ashore. For nine days, the war on Okinawa had belonged to infantry, artillery, and naval guns. What came next would add another dimension. From decks offshore, Corsairs prepared to cross the line between support and presence. The island had finished revealing its patience. Now it would demand endurance.

The launch came clean and hard. Corsairs leapt from the decks of the escort carriers in disciplined sequence, catapults slamming steel and flesh alike into the air. One after another the aircraft clawed free—VMF-312, VMF-322, VMF-323—96 Corsairs in total, wings heavy with ordnance, noses pointed west. The Pacific dropped away beneath them, the fleet already shrinking into something abstract and irrelevant.

Fred felt the familiar compression, the engine's steady violence under his right hand. No hesitation in the formation. No chatter on the radio beyond what was required. Everyone knew where they were going. Everyone knew the margin was thin. Kadena appeared quickly.

From altitude it looked finished enough to trust—a long scar of scraped coral edged by revetments and movement.

Engineers worked even as artillery walked lazily across distant ridges. Smoke hung low but didn't interfere. The pattern was open.

They landed without incident.

Figure 31. Corsair conducting catapult carrier launch.

Ninety-six aircraft touched down, cleared the strip, and disappeared into revetments hacked into the field's edge. No flak. No collisions. No aborted landings. For a moment, a moment—it felt as though timing alone had been on their side.

Fred taxied in, shut down, and climbed out into heat and noise that felt unlike anywhere he'd been before. This was not a base. It was a foothold.

\#

The ground echelon met them with tired efficiency. They had arrived the day before—stripped of everything

165

but people—building a camp without the equipment meant to make it possible. The men looked older than they should have. Canvas was hung where it could. Gear was arranged by necessity rather than design. There were no vehicles in neat rows. No supply stacks waiting to be inventoried. Nothing beyond what could be carried, begged, or salvaged.

Fred already knew why. With one part ashore, one part newly arrived, and the rest scattered somewhere behind the war, VMF-322 was not whole.

LST-599 had been gone six days. The ship carrying almost everything the squadron owned—fuel, food, water, ammunition, vehicles, tools, spare parts, the mess—had burned off Kerama Retto on April 3rd, ripped open by a kamikaze before it could unload. His people had survived by abandoning the ship with little more than personal gear.

The aircraft had arrived intact.

Everything beneath them had not.

Fred absorbed it without comment. He had already worked on the problem at sea. Now he was standing inside the consequences.

The days ahead would not separate cleanly. Patrols would bleed into strikes, strikes into emergency calls. Weather would stop them when the enemy could not.

That afternoon he gathered his senior enlisted men, including the Master Technical Sergeant, the Mess Sergeant, the Supply Sergeant, and the Maintenance Sergeant. They stood beneath a canvas ridge that barely deserved the name. Major J.R. Mathis stood with them, arms crossed, listening. There was no drama in the meeting. Only arithmetic.

"We don't have what we were issued," Fred said. "And we are not getting it on schedule."

No one argued.

"I want scrounging parties running around the clock," he continued. "Coordinate through J.R. and Operations. No one goes off alone. I don't care where it comes from. If it keeps our aircraft flying or men fed, we take it."

Mathis stepped in smoothly. "Borrow if you can. Trade if you must. Don't get stupid."

Fred nodded. "If anyone wants to know whose idea this is—it's mine." They broke immediately.

Figure 32. Marine fighting to move supplies in mud.

Small teams peeled off toward neighboring camps, dumps, abandoned Japanese positions—anywhere material might still be unclaimed. Tools appeared by evening that hadn't existed that morning. Fuel cans followed. Someone returned with a stove no one was willing to argue ownership over.

167

At night, under a single lantern, the three fighter squadron commanders met. They spoke plainly, without rank.

"Mission First, People Always," said Fred.

Sustainment came first—fuel prioritization, maintenance overlap, cannibalization rules. Defense followed—revetment spacing, field responsibility, what to do when Japanese artillery inevitably walked back onto Kadena. Intelligence was shared honestly: what was known, what wasn't, and how fast assumptions died here. All that, allowed Flight operations to happen.

MAG-33 would allocate and control who launched when, what could wait, and what could not. No one pretended to be independent.

"We hold this field together," Axtell said. "Or we don't hold it."

Day nodded once. "Runway's the bloodstream."

Fred leaned forward. "And we fly. Every day they ask us to. Even on days they don't. Because if we stop flying, the ground stops moving." They agreed without ceremony.

Figure 33. Kadena Airfield circle, 1945.

Outside, engines were already being run and shut down again, night crews working under blackout conditions, filling craters as fast as they appeared. Somewhere inland, guns answered other guns. The island gave nothing up easily.

By midnight, VMF-322 still had no proper mess. No reserve fuel worth trusting. No supply pipeline that could be relied upon. But it had aircraft.

It had men willing to build the rest from whatever could be pulled from the wreckage of a war that had no interest in fairness.

The scrounging reports were bleak: half rations. No spare magnetos. Barely enough fuel to promise a full day of flying. Fred stood over the supply tables while Mathis sorted through crates that didn't match their needs.

"We can play this tight," Mathis said. "Ground crews get less sleep. Aircraft get pushed harder. But we'll make the numbers."

Fred weighed it. He hated how reasonable it sounded.

Mathis watched him. "Or we slow the tempo and admit we can't keep up."

"That costs lives," Fred said.

Mathis nodded. "The other way costs our men."

Fred exhaled. "We'll do it the hard way."

Mathis closed the crate. "We usually do."

That shared burden—choosing the path that cost them both—settled between them without comment.

Alerts were sounded at **0502** and **1905**. No damage or casualties.

10 Apr 1945

Okinawa had taught everyone how the days would feel.

Only twenty-four sorties got up with negative results. **1Lt. Brown** from VMF-323 failed to return, listed as MIA. Remaining flights were cancelled due to bad weather and poor visibility.

One alert sounded at **0719**.

Figure 34. Major F. Rauschenbach- VMF 322

Figure 35. Major G. Axtell- VMF 323

Figure 36. Major Richard Day- VMF 312

11 Apr 1945

All flights cancelled.

Airstrip extremely soft, muddy and rutted due to heavy rain.

Alerts were sounded at **1021, 1340, 2050**

CHAPTER 37 — FIRST BLOOD

12 Apr 1945

Morning came already damaged. Enemy aircraft attacked at **0425** and **0530**.

Shelling then walked the field from **0800-0830** and again at **1435-1450**. Not with urgency, but with just enough accuracy to be devastating. VMF-312 had fourteen planes damaged and two from VMF-323 from friendly anti-aircraft fragments.

Figure 37. VMF-322 Corsair at Kadena Airfield.

A Service Squadron enlisted marine was critically injured and later died when stuck by a .50 caliber round.

Thirty-one aircraft scrambled at pre-dawn, downing three enemy aircraft. Forty-eight aircraft scrambled again at 1330, and downed twelve, two probably destroyed, and four damaged.

When Fred reached the line, smoke still rose lazily from revetments hit earlier. Aircraft sat slumped at angles no engineer ever planned for, wings bent, landing gear sunk into coral-turned-paste. Crew chiefs moved among them quietly, hands already blackened, saying nothing that wasn't necessary.

"Fourteen planes damaged from VMF-312," someone said.

"Two planes from 323," Fred said, nodding. There was relief in the numbers not being worse. He hated himself for it.

By mid-morning, planes were already being cannibalized. Damage assessed. Parts redistributed. No one asked when the next round would come. They all assumed it would.

They no longer began the days with anticipation. They began with inventory—aircraft that would start, pilots who could still fly, weather that might hold long enough to matter. Morning briefings shortened. There was little to explain, and no one needed persuasion. If an airplane could be made ready, it flew. If it could not, someone worked on it until it could.

VMF-322 settled into the rhythm without ceremony.

The sky was already crowded when Fred led his division off the strip.

Four Corsairs climbed eastward in loose echelon, engines settling into a steady, reassuring violence. Below them, the invasion fleet spread outward in layers—transports, escorts, radar pickets standing alone and brave at the edges of coverage. White wakes cut through dark water like chalk marks, each one vulnerable.

"Three-Two-Two Lead airborne. Climbing angels eight."

His wingmen answered in sequence. Calm. Professional. No wasted words. CAP over Okinawa punished lengthy comms. Warnings always come late.

They leveled and spread.

From altitude, the island looked deceptively still—patches of smoke inland, broken ridgelines, airfields scratched into coral. Offshore, ships moved with deliberate slowness, like targets refusing to acknowledge they were targets.

Fred scanned constantly. The threat was never where you expected it. Not above. Not ahead. It came low, skimming the water. Or high, out of cloud. Or staggered deliberately to overload attention.

Kamikaze pilots did not fight for air superiority. They fought for impact.

"Radar contact, bearing two-seven-zero," the controller said. *"Low and fast. Unknown number."* Fred tightened his formation.

"Division, push west. Keep spacing. We take the low one first."

They turned together, noses dropping slightly as airspeed built. Fred strained his eyes toward the shimmer between sea and sky, knowing how little contrast it took to hide something lethal.

"Visual," a wingman called. *"Single aircraft. Low. Japanese."*

The speck resolved too quickly—too low, too steady, closing on the fleet.

"No evasion," Fred said quietly. *"He's committed."* They dropped together.

The Corsair shuddered as Fred pushed into the dive, air speed climbing until the controls felt sharp again. Tracers arced up from ships below, desperate and scattered.

This wasn't a dogfight.

It was a timed intercept. Just being there when it mattered.

\#

That afternoon, Fred stood at the edge of the strip in the blue-black Okinawa dawn, headset around his neck, boots sinking into coral dust that never fully settled. Floodlights flickered where engineers fought to finish grading the runway. In the half-light, the Corsairs looked half-ghost, half predator—smoke curling, metal gleaming like wet bone.

Then came the warning, flat and unhurried over the field speakers:

"Enemy aircraft approaching from the west."

"Mount up!" Fred barked.

Pilots sprinted.

Tracers stitched the far side of the field as the first Japanese aircraft made a probing pass, its silhouette barely visible against the coming dawn. Marines dove for revetments. A mortar round landed behind the fuel dump, coughing coral into the air.

Fred leapt into his Corsair, slammed the canopy, signaled chocks out.

"322, Lead. Runway one-eight. Go. Go now."

The first Corsair lurched forward, tires carving bright lines through wet coral. A mortar burst near the northern service area, showering debris across the taxiway. Marines waved them on, ducking instinctively but never stopping.

Fred shoved the throttle forward. Torque bit hard, tail swinging wide.

"Easy ... easy ... " he muttered, forcing her straight.

Behind him, another aircraft nearly didn't make it. A near-hit rocked the ground mid-roll. The pilot overcorrected. The right wheel dug into soft coral left by the night rain.

"Lead—Two's hit—aircraft damage—taking her airborne"

Somehow, the Corsair clawed free, sparks spraying from the gear as it lifted.

Fred was already airborne.

"Form on me. CAP vector two-seven-zero," The controller cut in, tight and urgent:

"Multiple bogeys inbound—Judy and Tony. Out of Kerama Retto."

They broke through clouds and caught the glint—two silhouettes against the rising sun.

"Visual. Red Flight—Judy left. Blue Flight—Tony with me." Fred rolled into the dive.

The Tony came head-on, guns flashing. Tracers snapped past the canopy, close enough to vibrate the frame. Fred tightened his turn. His wingman slid into position and squeezed the trigger.

Six .50-calibers spoke as one.

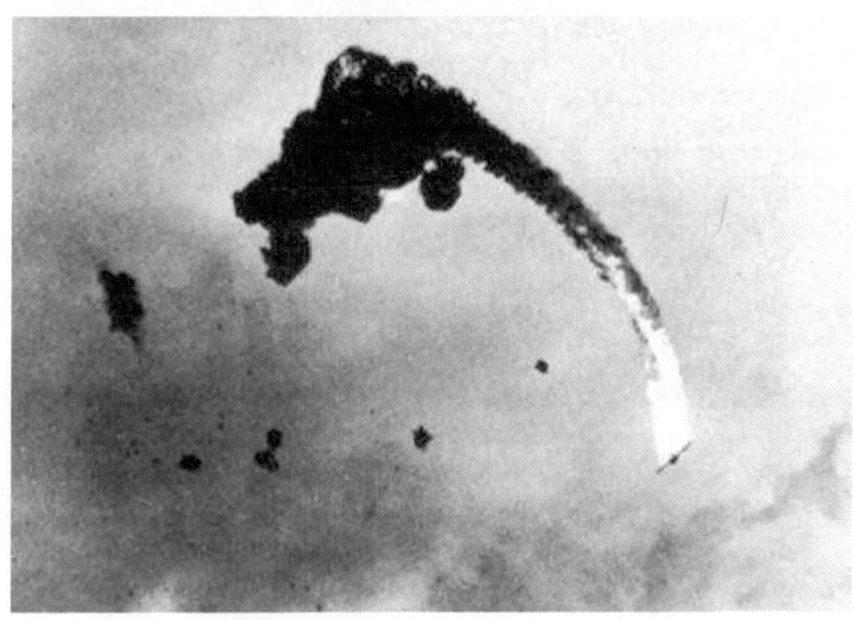

Figure 38. The burning sky claims Japanese dive bomber.

The Tony shuddered, smoke pouring from its cowling before it arced downward and vanished behind a ridge.

"Splash one Tony."

Red Flight finished the Judy moments later—two Corsairs crossing fire, the bomber tearing apart in burning fragments.

Below them, Kadena still burned. Mortars still fell. Marines still ran through fire.

But VMF-322 was airborne.

"Orbit and hold CAP," Fred ordered. *"Field remains hot."*

As dusk arrived fully, Okinawa revealed itself—craters, smoke, movement measured in yards.

Fred understood then: There would not be a single uncontested sortie on this island.

Figure 39. Corsair landing on Okinawa.

Debrief

The Corsairs had barely been tied down when Fred gathered pilots and key ground personnel beneath the half-standing maintenance tent. Cordite still hung in the air. Engineers shouted for sandbags near fresh craters.

178

Mathis stood beside him—calm, evaluating.

Johnson stood opposite, sleeves rolled high, grease and coral dust ground into his forearms, crew chiefs lined behind him.

Fred didn't raise his voice.

"You engaged two hostile aircraft. You splashed both. One aircraft damaged. No casualties. That's a solid start."

A mortar cracked beyond the ridge. The shockwave rattled loose metal.

No one flinched.

"You see why there's no easing into this."

A young pilot named Murphy finally exhaled. "Skipper … that was a Jesus Nut moment."

Mathis arched an eyebrow. "Explain."

Murphy swallowed. "It's when it hits you. Jesus, the nut is missing, Jesus, the tracers are real, or Jesus, those Tonys don't fly like silhouettes, and Jesus, this ain't practice anymore."

Mathis nodded once. "First real pass strips bad habits fast."

Fred didn't soften it. "Good. Hold onto that clarity. Everything on this island is trying to kill you—the enemy, the terrain, the weather, this field. Respect it, or it kills you."

Johnson stepped in without interrupting. "Mortar fires already bracketed the taxiway. We're dispersing aircraft, doubling berms, separating fuel and ammo. Aid station moved. Fire drills rehearsed."

Fred nodded.

"Pilots—listen to your crew chiefs. Ground—keep the line spread. Taxi spacing doubles until grading catches up." Johnson paused. "Treat every minute here like a Jesus Nut moment. Because it is."

Mathis clapped Murphy's shoulder. Johnson turned and barked orders. Above Kadena, clouds rolled in—heavy, dark, promising rain, mud, and more fire.

The first fight was over. Eighty-five sorties were flown by the squadrons. The war had begun.

Alerts were sounded at **0350,1330, 1455, 1900, 1930**.

13 Apr 1945 Disaster Hits

Pre-dawn light barely touched the coral strip as Fred's flight line came alive. Men moved with practiced economy, voices low, boots crunching softly over crushed coral still damp from the night. VMF-322 aircraft sat online, dark shapes waiting for the day to begin.

Fred was in Operations when the first Corsair rolled down the runway.

The engine sounded too eager. Wrong angle. Wrong pitch. Wrong altitude.

Torque hit instantly. The Corsair, one of VMF-323's, piloted by **2LT. Fountain**, during take-off veered and crossed the boundary between burning sky and ground. The aircraft yawed left, violently, the long nose swinging faster than correction could catch. The Corsair didn't lift. It lunged, skidding sideways off the strip and straight into VMF-322's parked aircraft.

It slammed into VMF-322's flight line. It had entered his space—his line, his men, his responsibility—the moment the throttle went forward.

The impact detonated the flight line. Metal tore through metal. A wing clipped the first Corsair, ripping it open, then slammed into another. Fuel tanks ruptured. Fire rolled outward, not upward, a horizontal wall of flame that swallowed revetments, tools, men.

The blast hit Fred in the chest before the sound did. Heat washed across the field in a single violent wave.

Smoke thickened instantly, tasting of burned rubber and aviation gas. Fred reached the edge of the line as fire crews arrived, forcing hoses into flame dense enough to feel solid. Ammunition cooked off sporadically, sharp cracks inside the roar. Aircraft that remained upright were dragged clear by hand until hands could no longer clutch hot metal.

The damage was worse than anyone wanted to say aloud.

Lt. Ronald T. Twitot never had time to react.

The aircraft disintegrated on contact, the cockpit crushed as the Corsair cartwheeled through Fred's line, scattering wreckage across the coral like shrapnel. There was no chance to run. No margin. Just violence.

M/TSGT Perry D. Johnson was on the line when it hit.

The best of Fred's men, one of the quiet ones who never drew attention and never left a job unfinished, he had been working between aircraft. The blast knocked him backward, fire catching immediately. Others ran toward him without thinking, but the heat drove them back. Fred saw it happen and knew—instantly—there would be no reaching him.

1Lt. Stanley Schlatter was closer still. He vanished in the first wave. Not thrown. Not burned later. Simply erased—replaced by wreckage, flame, and noise that drowned out everything else.

Three men from **Fred's squadron**. Gone in seconds.

James F. Mynatt, of VMF-323, was struck by a .50 caliber round while trying to extricate Lt. Schlatter from the scene of the crash and died shortly afterwards.

He reached the edge of the flight line as fire crews fought through heat that blistered skin and peeled paint from metal. Ammunition cooked off inside wreckage with sharp cracks that forced pauses no one wanted to take. Men dragged others clear by belts, by collars, by instinct.

When it ended, the strip looked flayed.

Three aircraft were destroyed. Three more damaged.

Three dead Marines that would not answer roll again.

Fred stood over Johnson longer. Johnson had been there from the beginning—quiet, competent, absolute. The squadron's spine. The man who made shortages survivable and discipline invisible. His death did not feel like loss. It felt like removal.

Three Corsairs were destroyed outright. Three more were damaged badly enough to be pulled from service. On a field that had started with too few aircraft, the math was immediate and unforgiving. No blame was assigned. No judgment could balance the equation. Okinawa had simply taken what it wanted early. Later, Fred sat alone beside a revetment long after the others had gone, a letter half-written in his lap. The words wouldn't come.

He didn't hear Mathis approach.

Mathis lowered himself beside him without speaking. For several minutes they sat in silence, broken only by distant engine tests and artillery inland.

After a few minutes, Mathis said, "We'll need to reassign men." It was not a dismissal but an acknowledgment.

Fred closed the letter. "Yeah. I know."

Mathis didn't leave. He didn't try to comfort. He just stayed. Only one man knew when Fred needed quiet instead of words.

Mathis, face blackened, voice raw. "Fred—"

"I want us airborne," Fred said.

It wasn't a decision. It was the only thing left.

Figure 40. A Marine consoles another Marine.

From that morning forward, Fred never watched a takeoff casually again. Every launch carried the memory of fire rolling sideways across his line—and of three men who never left the ground but paid the same price as those who fell from the burning sky: Twitot, Johnson, Schlatter, Mynatt.

Fred stood there while it happened, watching the chalk move, watching lines drawn through men he had eaten with, flown with, trusted. This was not enemy action. Not weather. Not chance. This was his flight line killing his people.

Field Farewell—Kadena Airfield

The wind shifted just before sunset, carrying smoke from burning brush piles across the northern edge of the field. The burning sky hung low and colorless, heavy with coral dust and the residue of explosions.

The war made no room for ceremony. They held one anyway.

Fred stood at the front of a rough semicircle—pilots in flight suits, crew chiefs with grease still on their arms, radio operators, ordnance men, clerks. Everyone who could be spared was there.

On three wooden crates draped with ponchos rested three helmets:

1st Lt. Stanley Schlatter—Communications Officer

2nd Lt. Ronald Twito—Aviator

Master Technical Sergeant Perry Johnson

Behind them stood three rifles, bayonets planted in coral.

Three sets of dog tags hung from the grips.

Three pairs of boots rested heel to heel.

Mathis stood beside Fred, jaw clenched hard enough to tremble. He had supervised the cleanup. He had seen what remained.

Johnson's dog tags tapped softly against the rifle stock in the breeze.

Fred removed his cover.

"Men," he said, his voice steady, despite the weight pressing down on him. "We are here to honor three of our own. Men who served this squadron—served each other—with loyalty and skill. Men who kept us flying when there were no guarantees."

He paused, eyes resting on Johnson's rifle a moment longer.

"This was an accident," Fred continued. "But they died in service to this squadron and this country. Their sacrifice is no different—and no less—than if it had happened while fighting the enemy." A murmur moved through the ranks.

"1st Lieutenant Schlatter kept our communications alive when they had every reason to fail. Second Lieutenant Twito flew with courage and discipline." He drew breath. "Master Technical Sergeant Johnson was the backbone of this squadron."

Mathis stepped forward, voice low and controlled.

"Johnson was the man every pilot trusted with his life. He fixed problems before we knew they existed. He fought for parts like he was fighting for breath." His jaw tightened. "When the rest of us were too tired to see straight, he held this unit together." No one moved.

From the rear, a Marine began the final muster.

"1st Lieutenant Schlatter." Silence.

"1st Lieutenant Stanley Schlatter." Heavier silence.

"1st Lieutenant Stanley Andrew Schlatter." The air itself seemed to sag.

The names of Mynatt and Johnson followed—each unanswered call landing like a blow.

From beyond the field came the low thump of outgoing artillery. The enemy did not care.

Fred replaced his cover. The Squadron was called to "Present Arms" Fred saluted, then the squadron was commanded to "Order Arms".

Fred dropped his salute, and solemnly commanded "Carry on."

They saluted as one, held it, then broke away—not because they were ready, but because the war demanded it.

Mathis remained beside Fred, staring at Johnson's helmet.

"He deserved better," Mathis said.

"We all do," Fred replied. "We just don't always get it." "How do we keep going?" Mathis asked.

Fred answered without looking away. "The same way they did. One mission at a time. This island, this enemy, this war . . . has hit us hard. But there is no quitting in this Squadron."

The CAP returned without incident.

No enemy. No contact. No answers.

Lt. Brown of VMF-323 had vanished days earlier, swallowed by the Pacific. Today it was Schlatter, Twitot, Mynatt, and Johnson.

It felt almost cruel to fly through the burning sky that had taken their friends and return to ground that was taking more. Loss was no longer an abstraction. It was becoming a tide.

The island did not pause for grief. Neither would they.

Commanders Meeting—Evening, 13 Apr

They met inside a half-standing tent that smelled of mud, kerosene, and exhaustion.

Axtell looked hollow. Day looked carved down to bone.

Fred felt older than he had any right to at twenty-four.

"Your man didn't survive," Day said quietly.

"Johnson?" Fred asked. "Lost all three," he replied shaking his head.

Axtell dragged his hand through his hair. "The pilot, Fountain, was mine. He tried to abort. He just—." He stopped. "He lost it."

"No blame," Fred said evenly. "Just consequence."

Rain hammered the canvas overhead. Outside, Marines shouted over incoming rounds, voices rising and falling with practiced urgency.

"Any resupplies making it in?" Axtell asked. "No," said Fred, shaking his head.

"Nothing yet, on resupply," Fred said. "Everything on 599 is at the bottom of the ocean. Everything we staged on the line is ash."

Day exhaled slowly. "You're flying like a full-strength squadron."

"We're not," Fred said. His voice didn't change. "We're only flying like one because we don't have any skin left on our teeth." No one argued. They all understood.

Alerts were sounded at **0315, 0400, 0835, 1800, 1930, 2125**.

CHAPTER 38 – CLOSE AIR SUPPORT (CAS)

12–21 Apr 1945, Machinato Line

By the time the Corsairs of VMF-322 launched to Kadena on the 9th of April, Kakazu Ridge had already turned malignant.

Below them, the 96th Infantry Division was locked into a geometry designed to kill methodically. Machine-gun pits buried under brush. Cave mouths blasted open only to reveal deeper chambers. Artillery firing from reverse slopes tanks could not climb, shells arcing out of invisible earth and vanishing back into it before counterfire could answer.

Nothing was forward.

Everything overlapped and interlocked.

VMF-322's first close air support runs were blind, fast, and violent.

\#

Rain arrived before dawn—warm, slanting sheets that pooled in bomb craters and turned taxiways into slurry. The field dissolved into mud and coral paste. Maintenance crews worked knee-deep, boots suctioned with every step, hands slick with rain and grease, improvising fixes that would have been unacceptable anywhere else.

Fred rolled his Corsair into a dive on a ridgeline marked only by a lone burning tree—an improvised reference passed up from scouts of the 7th Infantry Division, who had identified multiple machine-gun positions pinning down an entire battalion. There were no clean targets. Only probability.

Rockets slammed into the slope, tearing open firing pits that had never meant to be seen from above. Smoke and pulverized coral spiraled upward. Debris rained back down the hillside.

Infantry moved the instant the last rocket hit, climbing ground that had devoured men all morning.

Figure 41. Corsair unloads during a low-level CAS run.

It wasn't decisive. It wasn't permanent. But it bought minutes. On Kakazu, minutes were oxygen.

They did not stop.

VMF-322 flew two CAPs that morning—eight sorties total—screening the airspace while VMF-312 and VMF-323 guarded the fleet offshore. Fred remained in Operations during the second CAP, headset clamped tight, listening to clipped transmissions as fighters vectored and re-vectored against threats that often never materialized.

Enemy 152 mm shelling fell from **1545-1615**.

By early afternoon, the call came.

With only hours of light remaining, VMF-322 launched sixteen strike sorties—their first sustained offensive push since landing. Aircraft lifted off one by one through rain and smoke, engines straining against mud,

189

shortened margins, and five-hundred-pound bombs and
rockets.

The island answered everywhere.

Batteries fired inland.

Small arms crackled near the southern ridges.

Reports filtered in of Japanese infiltration attempts
near the airfields after dark—probing, patient, designed
to remind everyone that nowhere here was rear area.

By the time the last Corsair returned, daylight was
thinning fast. Mortar rounds began to walk toward
Kadena's perimeter, methodically and accurate, as if the
enemy had been waiting for nightfall all along.

At **1930**, an enemy aircraft strafed the runway,
damaging field lights.

That night, an Imperial Japanese Marine was
captured by squadron personnel and turned over to 24th
Army Corp MPs.

Alerts were sounded at 1000, 1120, 1925.
Scrounging parties never stood down. They moved
through Kadena and beyond it—trading labor for
equipment, equipment for fuel, fuel for time. Nothing
belonged to anyone long enough to feel ownership.

Pilots returned keyed tight, faces streaked with oil
and sweat, bringing fragments of the fight with them. CAS
bled into CAP. CAP gave way to emergency calls inland,
where infantry units found themselves pinned against
positions that did not exist on any map.

The Airfield

Kadena woke before light and stayed awake after
dark.

Enemy mortars and artillery shelled the airfield
constantly and without pattern. Engineers fought to keep
a usable runway alive. Engines turned over in half-
sequence, sometimes stopping again when fuel ran thin or
a part refused cooperation.

Seabees worked shirtless in rain, water sheeting down their backs, shovels striking mud more often than earth. Someone laughed once—hysterically—when a taxiway collapsed for the third time that night. No one joined in. Someone howled at the moon.

Figure 42. Constant enemy attacks forced Marines to seek cover.

Fred sent a flight to hit a ridge gap before weather closed in. It was the right call—until cloud rolled faster than forecast, visibility collapsing into dangerous uncertainty.

One pilot was disoriented. Another burned extra fuel repositioning. The sortie salvaged itself. Barely.

"Weather shifted early," Mathis said. "No one could've predicted it. We'll adjust spacing next time." No blame. No hesitation.

Fred caught the look—I fixed it; move on.

He did.

Later, when Mathis suggested reallocating two aircraft to another sector, Fred didn't question it. Balance restored. Trust reinforced.

The Night Crawlers

Work never stopped when shelling came. It merely paused.

Floodlights snapped off automatically as rounds landed close, plunging the field into darkness so complete, that men froze for fear of stepping on something broken or explosive. When impacts moved away, lights snapped back on and hands returned to tools without comment.

A mortar landed close enough to knock a man down. He stood, checked for blood, and went back to work. Kadena was not repaired. It was kept alive.

\#

Loss accumulated without announcement.

An empty revetment lingered longer than it should have. A name stayed on the board one day too long. A flight launched short a wingman and did not explain itself.

There was no dramatic break. Just subtraction.

VMF-312 and VMF-323 remained constant presences at the margins of Fred's days—voices on the radio, aircraft crossing altitudes, familiar silhouettes turning final. Sometimes they saved his pilots. Sometimes, his pilots saved theirs.

No one kept score. Team airpower was no longer a principle.

It was how the burning sky functioned.

The airfield took fire religiously. Artillery walked Kadena without pattern, shells arriving as reminders rather than attempts to shut it down. Crews scattered, returned, continued.

Aircraft were moved. Hit. Repaired. Moved again. Nothing stayed pristine long enough to deserve it.

Weather asserted itself daily, if not hourly. Rain turned coral into slurry and sealed ordnance into mud. Aircraft sat grounded while infantry called for support that could not reach them. Frustration rose and had nowhere useful to go.

Figure 43. Corsair on patrol.

When skies cleared, everything flew at once.

Those were the longest days. Sorties stacked back-to-back. Pilots flew until hands shook when they climbed down. Maintenance crews worked through meals and sleep, fixing damage just enough to risk it again.

Fred learned where to say yes—and where a delayed no would kill fewer men tomorrow.

14 Apr 1945—VMF-322 HQ's Midnight

The trucks arrived late.

Not from the village road but from the harbor side.

Fred was halfway through a maintenance status update when the sound carried in: engines straining, gears complaining under loads that had no business moving this far forward.

Someone leaned close and said quietly, "Sir. Supply just . . . arrived."

Two trucks rolled into view from the direction of the Navy harbor, where the invasion's logistical spine thrashed day and night under cranes, floodlights, and shouted inventories that never quite matched reality.

They were Navy trucks. Or had been, once. Both rode low, suspension pinned. Tarps were lashed down with rope borrowed from somewhere else entirely. Each vehicle dragged a water buffalo behind it, tanks swaying, liquid sloshing through the mud like a promise.

The Supply Sergeant climbed down first, boots caked to the knees, eyes rimmed red from something beyond fatigue. The Maintenance Sergeant followed more carefully, pausing to steady himself against the cab.

They snapped to attention.

"What is this?" Fred asked.

"Supplemental resupply, sir."

Fred walked the length of the first truck. Small arms ammunition stacked deep. Crates of food that weren't emergency rations. Uniform bundles. Sheets of plywood strapped along the sides. Spare parts scavenged across services, manufacturers, and logistics.

The second truck was worse.

Mess hall pots hung from the rails. Immersion heaters sat in open crates stenciled U.S. NAVY PROPERTY. Coffee tins. Sugar. Powdered milk. Enough to turn survival into function.

Fred stopped at the rear.

"Source?"

The Supply Sergeant's jaw set. Silence.

Fred waited.

The Maintenance Sergeant cleared his throat. "Sir. Naval invasion logistics. Harbor district."

Fred looked at him steadily. "You emptied a Navy staging site."

"No sir," the man replied evenly. "We participated in redistribution."

"Anyone complain?"

"Yes sir."

"And?"

"Strong objections were registered."

Fred nodded once. "And resolved?"

The Supply Sergeant answered. "Eventually, sir."

Behind them, a tarp lifted. Someone whistled softly—and stopped himself.

"Unload it," Fred said. "Quietly."

"Aye, sir."

Later, Mathis found Fred near Operations wearing a grin he hadn't worn since stateside.

"They left you something," he said, handing over two brown bottles.

Fred turned one slowly in his hand. Whiskey.

"One each," Mathis said. "For oversight."

"From whom?"

Mathis shrugged. "Let's call it appreciation for cooperation during a very educational evening."

They didn't drink it right away. They sat with their backs against an ammo crate that hadn't been there that morning, listening to generators hum and the harbor groan.

Later, they opened a bottle. Not much. Just enough. A whiff. A taste.

The next morning, coffee boiled in pots big enough to matter.

It didn't undo the deaths. It didn't stop the rain. It didn't soften April.

But for a few hours, the squadron functioned like something more than survivors.

Under invasion conditions, that was victory enough.

Alerts were sounded at **1000**, **1120**, and **1925.**

CHAPTER 39 – KAKAZU

15 Apr 1945

The briefing was shorter than it would have been a month earlier. Seemed intelligence you got on the ground didn't match what was fighting you in the air, or the marines were facing on the ground.

Fifty-three CAPs were flown, six enemy downed. **Lt. Zehring**, of VMF-323, didn't return. After destroying a Tony, he was seen flying into a hill immediately afterward. Two other VMF-323 planes were destroyed in landing accidents.

Pilots sat where they could—ammo crates, folding chairs, the ground itself—flight jackets open, helmets under arms, faces worn beyond their years. A map was tacked to plywood with nails that bent as often as they held. Red grease pencil marked ridges that meant nothing until someone tried to cross them.

Figure 44. Two Marines engage the enemy.

Fred stood in front of it without preamble. "Chocolate Drop Hill," he said, tapping the map with two fingers. "And everything tied to it is now the fight."

"Three missions, 43 sorties," he said. "Ordnance mix of 500-pound-bombs, rockets."

No one needed that translated.

"The ground forces hit it hard earlier this week. Artillery didn't break it. Naval gunfire didn't break it. What they found instead was a line that doesn't announce itself." He drew a shallow curve along the map. "Reverse slopes. Saddles. Caves that don't look like caves until they open fire." A pilot leaned forward. Another closed his eyes, listening.

"This is not a single objective," Fred continued. "This is the front of Shuri Line. Same ground, different grid squares. Expect to hit it more than once. Expect yesterday's target to look dead until it isn't. He let that sit.

"What they need from us isn't heroics. It's time. Suppression long enough for movement. Smoke where they can't get it themselves. Runs close enough to matter."

Someone asked the question without raising a hand.

"How close?" Fred didn't soften it.

"Too close for comfort. If you aren't uncomfortable, you're probably too high. Don't pull up until the green turns to grass." No smiles.

"You'll hear FACs who know what they want and others who are learning fast. When they say danger close, believe them. When they ask you to hold fire, do it. When they clear you hot, don't waste the window." He scanned the faces.

"You won't always see what's shooting at them. That doesn't mean it isn't there. If fire stops after your first pass, don't assume it's done. They're patient. We have to be even more so." Fred stepped back.

"VMF-312 and VMF-323 are working the same ground. You'll hear them on frequency. Cover each other. If someone goes Winchester or takes hits, another squadron finishes the job." That landed.

"Bring the aircraft back," he finished. "Bring each other back. If we bend the ridge enough for them to move, we've done our job."

The briefing ended without dismissal. Pilots stood, adjusted gear, drifted toward aircraft already ticking warm. Outside, the weather held just long enough to make the first launch worth trying.

Fred stayed by the map, eyes still on Chocolate. He knew they would be back over it tomorrow, and the day after that. The airfield was bombed, strafed, and shelled throughout the day.

\#

16 Apr 1945

The enemy 152mm guns opened at **0330** and the barrage lasted an hour. VMF-312 had one KIA **M/TSGT Huyteus**, three wounded, three planes destroyed and one damaged. Everyone and everything paid a price. Eighty-eight CAP missions were flown, and eleven enemy aircraft destroyed. Two pilots bailed out at sea but were rescued.

Alerts sounded at **0215, 0945, 1920, 2050**.

Close Air Support — Kakuza Ridge

The ridge did not look like it was defended from the air.

That was how it always began.

Four Corsairs circled low over the western edge of the Machinato/Shuri Line, engines steady, noses down just enough to feel the pull. Smoke from earlier bombardment lay thin and deceptive, broken only by dark seams where artillery had peeled soil back to rock. The call from the ground came clipped and tight.

"Any aircraft, this is Red Two-One. We're pinned on the east face. Multiple guns. Cannot locate visually."

Fred leaned closer to the radio.

Figure 45. Two Marines advance on Wana Ridge.

"Red Two-One, this is Navy Three-Two-Two. Roger. Stand by." The FAC came up seconds later, voice steady but economical.

"They're in there. Reverse slope. Caves. Fire cuts off whenever we get eyes."

Fred watched his lead aircraft peel off, nose dipping as the Corsair slid down through broken clouds.

"I'm taking fire," the pilot said calmly. *"Tracers up the ridge line. Marking."*

A plume of white smoke bloomed where nothing had been seconds earlier. *"There,"* the FAC said. *"Danger close. Infantry one hundred yards north."* That collapsed the world to inches.

"Cleared hot."

The Corsair rolled in. The whistle arrived before the guns, air screaming across metal as .50-caliber fire stitched the ridge face. Dust erupted. Tracers answered briefly—then stopped.

The second aircraft followed with rockets, firing into the same scar without ceremony.

The ridge went quiet. It stayed quiet long enough.

Below, men moved—figures rising from cover that had held them for hours, stretchers coming out, squads shifting forward in ones and twos. Fred tracked the clock without looking at it.

Quiet never lasted.

"Secondaries firing," the FAC warned. *"Same grid. Same mouth. Repeat."* Napalm took it on the third pass.

The fire clung where bombs never did, rolling into seams and openings artillery could not reach.

"Fire slackening," the FAC said. *"Infantry moving."* That was the best outcome they hoped for.

No cheers followed. The flight stayed overhead until fuel forced a decision, then peeled off one by one, engines already running hotter than they should have.

As the last Corsair climbed, fire flickered again from somewhere deeper in the ridge.

Fred exhaled slowly. They had not taken Kakazu. But they had bent it—just enough. Four VMF-322 planes were damaged by enemy AA.

17Apr 1945

0130hr- **Lt. Iverson** VMF(N)-543, was killed during a night take-off accident.

Airfield strafed.

18 Apr 1945

Exhaustion had settled into the squadron like humidity. Not sharp. Not dramatic. Just present. 48

CAS/32 CAP sorties launched. The ground still moved forward when air support arrived on time. The enemy still resisted without exposing himself. Nothing suggested climax or collapse.

This was not a campaign that would be decided quickly. It was decided by increments small enough to survive. Fred walked the line each evening as engines ticked cool, counting aircraft by instinct. Fewer now. But enough. Still enough.

One alert sounded at **1945** with no damage.

19 Apr 1945

Rain and wind. Minimal sorties.
Alert sounded at **1945.**

20 Apr 1945

VMF-322 lost a plane to A.A. fire. Pilot was rescued. The squadron had not broken. On Okinawa, that counted as progress.

Kadena Airfield was again shelled by enemy 152mm artillery from **0330-0420.**
One moment the field was loud with engines and shouted instruction, the ordinary chaos of Kadena finding its rhythm. The next, it went quiet in the wrong way—the kind of quiet that meant aircraft were moving fast where they shouldn't be. Someone yelled.
The strafing run came without warning that same evening at **1845** hrs. No alert.
Tracers cut across the perimeter in a clean red line, deliberate and level, forcing men flat more from instinct than training. The attack lasted close to two hours. No one counted them. When it was over, two vehicles burned and a fuel bladder leaked slowly enough to matter. No aircraft

were hit. Five men were injured by fragmentation bombs, machine gun strafing.

That was recorded as success.

\#

By late April, the faces began to change. Not all at once. Not dramatically. One pilot rotated out. Another arrived half-trained and eager. A third disappeared from the board and never reappeared. The squadron absorbed it the way it absorbed everything now —quietly, without comment—adjusting rosters until continuity returned in a thinner form.

Fatigue showed first at the margins. Pilots checked each other's work without being asked. Maintenance chiefs enforced stand-downs before hands shook badly enough to matter. Men slept where they could and learned to wake instantly to engine noise that might carry their name with it. Exhaustion crept into places no enemy ever could.

Two men were wounded by their own squadron physician when they failed to halt fast enough in the dark. Flesh wounds. No charges. Just another sign of nights without sleep and reflexes worn thin.

Two alerts sounded at **0430** and **1940**.

21 Apr 1945

The ridges did not change. Another spur south of Kakazu—rockier, sharper, cut deeper by artillery—took its turn becoming the focus. It had a name that mattered only on maps and in casualty reports. To the men flying it, it was simply that ridge again. Others knew it as "Hacksaw Ridge."

Figure 46. Low level CAS support.

The call language sounded familiar now. Armed recon. Immediate CAS. Repeat. Danger close.

Fred listened from Operations as the flight checked in, four Corsairs sliding into a low orbit, engines already hot from the climb. The FAC's voice carried strain even before the first call for fire. *"They're waiting today,"* he said. *"Heavy guns."*

The first aircraft rolled in and the burning sky answered. Anti-aircraft fire rose hard and organized, black bursts walking toward the dive path with an intelligence that felt personal. Tracers stitched past the Corsair's wings, forcing a pull-out early and crooked.

"I'm hit," the pilot said, his voice flat. He stayed airborne.

The second run came lower and faster. Rockets left the rails cleanly and disappeared into rock that erupted without revealing what it had swallowed. Fire slackened for seconds—then surged again from a different angle.

"*Taking more,*" another voice reported. "*Controls sluggish.*" Fred felt the pattern closing.

This wasn't suppressive fire meant to harass. It was deliberate. Ranged. Patient.

The third aircraft took a hit climbing out. Smoke trailed briefly, then broke into something worse. The pilot's transmission cut short, then returned—thin, controlled.

"*I'm going for the water.*"

Silence followed—long enough to feel like loss. "*Chute's out.*" Someone exhaled near the radio without realizing it.

Two Corsairs limped back toward Kadena, skins torn, systems compromised, damage already being tallied in minds that never stopped counting. One would fly again after nights of work. One would not. The destroyed aircraft's absence felt immediate.

The pilot was recovered hours later by a Navy boat whose crew had been listening for that exact call.

Figure 47. VMF-312 Corsair gets re-armed.

Back at Kadena, Fred watched the flight board change shape again.

Three aircraft damaged. One gone. One pilot safe, wet, finished for the day. The math tightened.

That night, the squadron absorbed the day the way it now absorbed everything—by continuing. Replacement pilots checked in quietly. Veterans flew again with smaller margins. Maintenance crews worked into darkness that had long since stopped feeling threatening.

The ridges remained. So did the work.

Fred stood by the line, counting aircraft by habit, knowing how close the day had come to taking something it could not afford to lose. The war had shifted again—not in violence, but in density. Fire heavier. Days longer. Rest shallower.

April was running out. The men were not. Not yet.

Command Ground Vs. Air

At altitude, Fred knew exactly who he was.

The cockpit sealed around him like a promise—engine steady, wings clean, controls alive under his hands. The war simplified immediately.

Airspeed. Angle. Formation spacing. Threat. Break. Reform.

Command in the air was intimate. Four aircraft. Four voices. No arguments. No delays. Decisions arrived fully formed and were paid for immediately. If he led them wrong, he died with them. If he led them right, they moved as one, the burning sky bending just enough to let them through.

Up there, tomorrow did not exist. Only the next seconds mattered. In the air, his mistakes killed quickly. Radios speaking in fragments. Mathis at his shoulder, asking questions whose answers would land on men who trusted him absolutely.

On the ground, Fred could not maneuver. On the ground, tomorrow never stopped existing. He had to decide. Who flew again. Who waited. Who rested. Who never would.

On the ground, they killed slowly. Here command spread outward, thickened, slowed. Every choice dragged a future behind it: aircraft readiness boards, pilot fatigue charts, weather windows closing. Maintenance chiefs with problems that could not be solved—only managed.

The burning sky let him escape responsibility. The earth made him absorb it.

No damage resulted from alerts at **0050**, **2000**, and **2040**.

CHAPTER 40 – MEATGRINDER

Life began to blur.

Shelling walked across Kadena and made a mockery of preparation. Aircraft sat crippled in their revetments—or were bulldozed out to the "Bone Yard"—machines damaged not by skill or intent, but by proximity. Repairs began immediately, because they had to. No one asked whether the field would be shelled again. They worked as if it would.

Two days later, word moved fast through Operations. **Captain Johnson of VMF-312** had taken four aircraft into a swarm and come back with fewer enemies in the burning sky than he'd found. The numbers varied—eight, ten—but no one doubted the effect. For the first time in days, it felt as if the air might tilt. The optimism didn't last.

Then the air changed again.

22 Apr 1945

VMF-323 met the enemy in numbers—and for once held every advantage. Seven Corsairs against a flaming sky full of Japanese aircraft—thirty-five by some counts. When it ended, more than twenty-five enemy planes were gone. The word **"Turkey Shoot"** appeared for the first time, spoken without celebration. Three aces were made that day: Dorrah, Axtell, O'Keefe. No one lingered on the honor. There were missions to fly.

The following day, a VMF-322 pilot struck a bulldozer on landing, wrecked a wheel and an aileron, stayed airborne on stubbornness alone, and then bailed out over the sea. The **USS St. George** pulled him from the water cold and breathing.

It had been about surviving long enough to earn it.

Kakuza Ridge

The ridge didn't look different this time. Fred led the division in low, following scars left by yesterday's strikes. Smoke climbed unevenly, sun glare flattening depth perception until rock and shadow blurred together.

They rolled in one by one. Heavy fire rose immediately, disciplined, accurate. Tracers stitched past Fred's left wingtip, close enough to read intent. He held his line, waited for the clearance, then fired. Rockets left the rails clean. The Corsair shuddered through turbulence and blast wash. Fire chased him briefly on the pull-out, then settled back into the ridge as if nothing had happened. Another pass. Then another. Suppression long enough for movement below.

That was the work. Fuel forced the return. Damage assessment came later. One aircraft limped home with control issues with another diverted to Yontan. None were lost this time. That counted. Fred landed with his jaw set, climbed out without ceremony, already halfway into the next problem before the engine was fully wound down.

Mathis met him near Operations. "Replacements are in," Mathis said. "Three pilots."

Fred nodded. "Let's brief them."

They stood beneath netting strung too low to be comfortable. The new men looked clean by comparison—eyes bright, gear intact, names still unscarred by repetition.

Fred didn't soften it. "You're here because we fly every day," he said. "Because the grunts need us. Because Okinawa doesn't allow pauses." He pointed toward the flight line, met their eyes, one at a time.

"You'll lead when I tell you. You'll follow when I tell you. You'll break off when you're ordered—even if you think you can finish the run. We don't get points for staying one pass too long." No one asked questions.

Fred dismissed them and watched as they moved toward aircraft that already felt heavier than they had an hour ago. Mathis stayed. "Hell of a day," he said. Fred nodded once.

He looked back toward the ridges, already accepting that tomorrow would look much the same. Up there, he could still fly. Down here, he had to keep the squadron alive long enough for flying to matter. Both demanded everything. Neither offered relief.

No damage from two alerts sounded at **0140** and **1824**.

23 Apr 1945

The weather returned. It didn't fall. It inserted itself. Rain came sideways at first, then fell straight down, rebounding upward from the coral until direction stopped meaning anything at all. Mud swallowed ankles, then boots, then whole legs if you stood still too long. Men learned to walk without lifting their feet, dragging them free a fraction at a time. Nothing stayed dry long enough to pretend it mattered. Kadena began to disappear.

Taxiways collapsed into soap. Aircraft settled nose-low into ground that had been solid hours earlier. Crews waded chest-deep, hauling equipment by rope and curse, wrapping engines in canvas that soaked through before it could help.

Most of those strikes went unnoticed beyond the ground units that survived them. Pilots returned filthy. Aircraft came back and shot through. Fuel burned down to margins that made no one comfortable. There were no announcements. No ceremonies. Just the next call. And then the next.

24 Apr 1945

Rain and mud made Kadena runways unusable. Fred watched two planes nose over during landings and changed course. all flights canceled, all flights to operate from Yontan Airfield. Three Corsairs were damaged and one was destroyed. The math tightened again. Sleep came in fragments. Men lay down fully dressed, boots on, helmets within reach. No one bothered with using tents that wouldn't keep out rain or shrapnel.

Fred learned to wake instantly at the sound of incoming, his body moving before thought caught up. Shelling continued without enthusiasm—as if even the enemy understood endurance mattered more than accuracy now.

Some nights the guns came every hour. Other nights they didn't, which was worse. Someone began counting rounds out loud until another man told him to stop.

Figure 48. Nighttime defensive fire tracers.

Fred made a note on the board at dawn, erased half of it later when daylight revealed new damage. He drank coffee boiled from a pot that hadn't been there yesterday and tried to remember the last time the ground hadn't moved beneath him. April was no longer about invasion. It was about endurance.

\#

Japanese shelling arrived just often enough to erase rhythm—too irregular to predict, too consistent to ignore. When a round landed close, the ground jumped before the sound reached you. When nothing landed, the waiting pressed harder than fear.

That night, floodlights clawed at the dark. Seabees worked beneath them without pause, shovels biting water more often than earth. When artillery walked closer, the lights snapped off—then back on again as soon as the impacts passed. Construction didn't stop. It adapted. Fred moved through it wrapped in a poncho that stopped nothing. Mud fought every step. He checked revetments, nodded at men beyond encouragement, made decisions that all reduced to the same thing. Keep moving. Keep flying. Don't let the field die.

26 Apr 1945

Just before midnight, a shell found the flight line. It wasn't precise. It didn't need to be. The Corsair nearest the revetment took the blast cleanly. Fire raced through fuel and metal before anyone could reach it. Three nearby aircraft were torn open—control surfaces shredded, cowlings peeled back, shrapnel buried deep enough to make tomorrow uncertain.

Crews charged anyway. Their hoses dragged through mud that stole momentum.

Figure 49. Damage from enemy attack.

Fire hissed and steamed and finally collapsed in on itself, leaving wreckage and the smell of scorched oil hanging low over the field. No one spoke.

By dawn, the rain still hadn't stopped. Men leaned against aircraft they could no longer fly and slept standing up. Others worked because stopping meant noticing how much everything hurt.

Fred stood at the edge of what passed for a runway—flooded, gouged, barely functional—and thought briefly of clear skies he no longer trusted. The war was not advancing that night. It was persisting. So were they.

There was one alert at **0225** and at **0330** enemy shells landed. No injuries.

27th Apr 1945

Weather broke. All 3 squadrons took on the burning sky, flying 121 CAP sorties and 16 CAS sorties. The Battle of the Maeda Escarpment (Hacksaw Ridge) had begun yesterday. At **0310** enemy shelling began.

Three alerts were sounded at **0217**, **2045**, and **2342**.

28th Apr 1945

The ridge had pinned Company G, 383rd Infantry Regiment, 96th Infantry Division since morning. It wasn't high—nothing dramatic—but it rose just enough to give the enemy everything they needed. Fire came from places that didn't look like firing positions. When one gun went quiet, another opened thirty yards away, precise and patient. Men learned quickly which patches of ground would kill them and which merely threatened to.

By mid-afternoon, no one was moving. A platoon sergeant pressed his helmet into the dirt and keyed the handset again, voice flattened by repetition. *"George Six, requesting immediate air. Grid follows."* He didn't look up when he finished. He stared at a boot half-buried in mud and wondered briefly whether it had been his once. The minutes stretched. Shells cracked overhead. Someone behind him vomited quietly and wiped his mouth with the back of his hand.

Then the sound changed. It came first as vibration, not noise—low, rolling, different from artillery or naval guns. The ground felt it before the ears did. "Aircraft inbound," someone shouted, unnecessarily.

The Corsairs appeared through broken clouds, dark shapes piercing holes in the burning sky. They came in low enough that the infantry could see the undersides of their wings, the round insignia smeared with oil and dust. They did not circle. They did not linger.

Smoke popped on the slope where the forward observer wanted it—close enough to make everyone flinch. *"Danger close,"* the FAC said. The lead aircraft rolled in.

But the strike was off from the moment it began.

The dive angle was wrong—or the wind shifted—or the pilot had one second less visibility than he needed. The rounds struck high, chewing harmless rock. The explosion blew dust outward in a clean halo— impressive and useless.

The second Corsair tried to correct but overcompensated. Fire walked behind the target, nowhere near the cave mouth. The machine gun answered immediately, untouched.

Someone swore. Someone else said nothing at all.

"Negative effect," the platoon sergeant said into the handset. *"Repeat. I say again, Negative effect."* The Corsairs were already pulling out, low and fast. One of them wobbled—just enough to make men look up instead of forward. The pilot caught it, barely, and disappeared toward the sea. The ridge did not change. The two men out front remained where they had fallen.

At dusk, when the line had moved thirty yards and stopped again, the lieutenant wrote in his notebook that air support had achieved excellent results. What he meant was this: Everyone who could walk still was alive. Tomorrow, they might move another thirty.

After Action Report—Kadena CP

Fred saw the Corsair coming in too fast long before it reached the strip. The aircraft wavered on approach, wings dipping unevenly, prop wash shuddering through air thick with humidity. Ground crew ran. Someone shouted for crash trucks. Radios barked instructions that went unanswered. The pilot fought it all the way down.

The wheels touched, bounced, touched again. The aircraft slewed left, corrected sharply, and rolled to a stop halfway down the strip. Exhaust coughed in ragged pulses before the engine finally died. Fred was moving before the prop stopped turning.

The canopy slid back. The pilot sat there for a moment, his head bowed, hands gripping the coaming like he needed the aircraft to stay still long enough for the world to stop spinning. When he finally looked up, his eyes found Fred immediately.

"I missed it," he said.

Not an excuse. A verdict.

Fred reached the wing and steadied the pilot as he climbed down. His legs shook when they hit the ground— not from fear, but the kind of adrenaline that leaves no room for breathing.

"Wind changed on the run," the pilot said. "Or I was late. Or early. I couldn't see the smoke until I was committed." He swallowed. "There were friendlies close. I pulled too far left." He looked away, jaw set. "I don't know what happened to them."

Fred didn't interrupt. There wasn't a clean answer because there wasn't a clean outcome.

"It happens," Fred said quietly.

The pilot shook his head once. "It shouldn't."

Men were gathering now—crew chiefs, mechanics, men with nothing official to do except witness the cost no report would record. The Corsair's underside showed fresh coral gouges where the dive had gone too low. A single round hole sat in the wing root, clean through, dangerously close to the fuel tank.

Fred rested a hand on the pilot's shoulder. "You flew it home." The pilot gave a tired laugh with no humor in it. "That's the part I'm not proud of." Fred understood.

The failure wasn't the miss. It was surviving it.

Four alerts were sounded at **1116**, **1605**, **1930**, and **2030**.

29th Apr 1945

The morning's 152mm artillery barrage was on target. 1 plane destroyed and 3 damaged. The call came late in the afternoon, when the light went flat and depth perception lied.

Grid numbers followed—tight, familiar. A ridge that had resisted movement since morning. Infantry dug shallow, waiting for daylight to run out. Enemy fire organized but not ambitious—the kind that killed steadily rather than dramatically.

Fred looked down the flight line. Four aircraft were ready. Not perfect. Nothing was anymore. But flyable. Armed. Fueled to margins he trusted. "Four-plane division," he said. "My lead. We are joining up with 312 on this run."

They launched with the field still damp from the last rain, gear retracting unevenly as Corsairs clawed into air heavy with moisture. Fred took them low immediately, skimming beneath cloud cover that pressed down like a ceiling meant to keep men honest.

"Two, check in."
"Two is up."
"Three?"
"Three."
"Four?"
"Four."

He brought them in from the south, using ridges he'd memorized by feel rather than map.

The FAC's voice came tight but steady. *"Friendlies danger close. Marking now."* Smoke bloomed where it mattered.

Fred rolled first. The sight picture locked clean—ridge line centered, cave mouth visible only because he'd learned to recognize absence as well as shape. He held the dive one breath longer than comfort allowed, then fired. The Corsair shook as .50 calibers rockets followed, punching into rock and dirt where fire had come from all day. He pulled out low, wings clearing the slope with nothing to spare. "*One away,*" he said.

The second aircraft rolled in immediately, stitching the ridge with precision born of repetition rather than confidence. The third hit slightly left, suppressing rather than destroying—exactly as intended. The fourth came in fast and low, guns hammering the draw where tracers had risen minutes earlier. Anti-aircraft fire answered, thin now. Desperate.

Rounds snapped past Fred's canopy on the climb out, one striking close enough to ring through the airframe. He ignored it. Checked his mirrors. Watched the rest of his division clear clean.

"*Good effect,*" the FAC said. Then, quieter: "*We're moving.*"

Fred circled once more, unwilling to leave until the infantry confirmed ground gained. Smoke drifted. Fire stayed silent. "*Roger,*" he said. "*Holding.*"

When they finally turned back toward Kadena, fuel gauges sat where he'd expected them to—low, honest, unforgiving. No one spoke on the ride home.

Back on the field, crews moved in practiced silence—counting holes, checking control surfaces, hands steady from experience rather than rest. One Corsair showed shrapnel scarring along the belly. Another leaked oil slowly enough to pretend it wasn't serious.

Next day, a bewhiskered group of infantry walked into the VFM-322 CP. "*We're looking for the pilots that flew over that ridge yesterday. We got something for them.*"

They came bearing gifts- rifles, flags, wrist watches, lockets, and medals. Souvenirs most pilots would never get a chance to bring home.. It was the infantry's gesture of thanks.

Alerts were sounded at **0425**, **2105**, **2123**, and **2330**.

\#

By the final week of April, the fight slid west toward terrain that refused abstraction: Sugar Loaf Hill, Horseshoe, Half-Moon. Ground that later in May shredded entire companies of the 6th Marine Division and made casualty figures feel dishonest.

The Marines signaled for air.

Fred flew his Corsairs low enough to see helmet colors below—green and brown shapes pressed flat against the slope, pinned by sniper fire and mortars buried deep into limestone that swallowed punishment and gave nothing back.

The Corsairs lined up their runs, rockets punching into the Horseshoe's rock face. Stone exploded outward. Dust and debris rained down over defenders long enough to matter.

It wasn't enough to take the hill. But it kept Marines from dying where they lay.

By Okinawa's measure, that counted.

After returning from the mission, Fred taxied and shut down last. As he climbed down, the sun bled out behind the ridges they'd just left, the burning sky reddening not from fire but from the simple mechanics of evening.

April was finished. It had taken aircraft and men and deprived them of sleep.

What it had given in return was thinner. Ground taken. Lines on the map moved. Across the month, two hundred and ninety-two close air support strikes were flown—low, measured, repetitive work carried out under cloud ceilings that flattened the burning sky and anti-aircraft fire that never quite disappeared.

No single mission stood out. None were meant to.

They hit ridges already struck and still resisting. Cave mouths that fell silent long enough for infantry to move and then spoke again. Reverse slopes artillery couldn't reach. Machine-gun nests that mattered only because men were pinned beneath them.

By the end of the month, the numbers told one story for MAG-33:

Seventy-eight enemy aircraft destroyed, eight probable, and eleven damaged.

Enemy contact on only seven days out of nineteen flown.

The men who lived it knew better. April hadn't been about dominance.

The results were recorded as excellent—a word that meant something very specific to the people asking for help. It meant someone moved who hadn't been able to. It meant casualties came back instead of staying forward. It meant a line bent instead of breaking.

Figure 50. Marines on the trench line.

CHAPTER 41 – MAY 1945

My dear Fred,

I don't know where you are exactly when this reaches you, so I'll avoid assumptions. I imagine heat. I imagine noise. I imagine you reading this briefly, somewhere that isn't meant for sitting.

Things here continue the way they always do—forward, regardless of how anyone feels about it. Days fill themselves. Men come and go. Some leave more quietly than when they arrive. I'm learning how to recognize which ones need conversation and which only need to know someone noticed them.

I'm careful not to ask questions in letters. The answers take too long, and imagining is rarely correct. Instead, I'll say only that I hope you're eating when you can, sleeping when the opportunity presents itself, and letting other people do their jobs as well as they know how.

You once told me delegation was a form of trust. I've been thinking about that. Baltimore feels very far away now. I don't miss it the way I expected to. I miss specific things instead—familiar hands, familiar voices, knowing where the day is likely to end. I don't tell anyone that. They wouldn't know what to do with it.

When I walk at dusk, the light still surprises me. I think of the way you look at the fiery sky—not as something beautiful, but as something to be understood. I find myself doing the same thing now, though I doubt our reasons are alike.

I won't make this longer than it needs to be. I only wanted you

to know that I think of you often, and not idly. There's a difference, even at this distance.

Take care of yourself, Fred. In the ways that matter most.

Elaine

Figure 51

CHAPTER 42 – THE 3RD ECHELON

April is finally over. The MAG-33 total stood at 19 total flight days. Enemy contact during only seven days.

VMF 312- lost six planes and one KIA.

VMF 323- lost four planes and two KIA.

VMF 322- lost six planes and three KIA, plus all supplies and equipment on LST-599.

1344 **CAP** sorties, plus 140 by the night squadron. Resulted in 79 kills, 8 probable's, 11 damaged. 292 **CAS** strikes, excellent results.

01 May 1945—0700Z

The **USS Sea Bass** arrived without ceremony.

At first light she eased into position off Okinawa Shima, another gray shape among too many to count. For the men aboard, the approach felt anticlimactic—no sound of guns close enough to measure, no clear sense yet of where the island began and ended. Just coastline, low and indistinct beneath cloud that refused altitude.

The third echelon stood on deck and waited. Seventy-four enlisted men and two officers. **First Lieutenant Sydney Jenkins**— called "I" without explanation and without argument—stood at the rail and watched the shore as if he were already calculating what would be lost between ship and sand. They had trained for months to arrive ready. They had not trained to arrive late.

Boats took them in by stages. Gear followed slowly, some of it newer than what waited ashore, some already obsolete by the sound of distant impacts that began registering before anyone admitted they were hearing them. The harbor smelled of fuel, wet steel, and something burned into the air that no one tried to identify.

The first incoming round landed inland. No one flinched. The second landed closer.

This one they felt. It knocked conversation out of mouths and pressed it back into chests where it stayed. Jenkins turned and shouted for spacing, for movement, for speed without panic. His voice carried better than most—cutting through the soundscape like something already practiced. By mid-morning they reached Kadena. What they saw rearranged expectations immediately.

Aircraft sat in pieces that looked intentional until you stood close enough to recognize violence. Revetments were deeper than doctrine. Taxiways ended abruptly where the earth had simply given up. Men moved through mud without comment, doing work that never seemed to finish before the next shell bracketed the field again. Someone laughed once—short, sharp—and then stopped.

The enlisted men of the Supply Echelon took it in without being told what to think. This wasn't the front line they had imagined. It was worse. There was no edge to it. No boundary where danger politely waited to be invited. A mortar landed close enough to make that clear.

By noon, Jenkins had them working. Crates were opened. Inventories checked against lists that no longer meant what they were written to mean. The men learned quickly that being supply on Okinawa did not mean distribution—it meant triage. Everything went somewhere. Nothing went everywhere.

Decisions were made by people whose job descriptions did not include deciding what would matter most tomorrow. Morale adjusted. There was no collapse. No ceremony. Just a narrowing of conversation and a seriousness that did not lift again. Someone quietly said that the pilots looked exhausted. Someone else replied that exhaustion appeared to be the baseline.

That evening shelling walked the perimeter again. The Supply Echelon learned where to lay flat and where not to bother. They learned which sounds came before impact and which came after. They learned that the work did not stop because the guns started. It paused long enough to count. When darkness fell, Jenkins walked the perimeter once, checking his men with nods instead of words. No speeches. No reassurances. They didn't need them. They had arrived.

Okinawa had acknowledged receipt.

#

The improvement did not happen all at once. It arrived in waves—uneven, delayed, occasionally misdirected—but it arrived all the same. Within days, replacement supplies from Guam began working their way forward, ferried in by ships that did not linger and men who did not ask what had been lost to make room for what remained. Crates appeared bearing stencils that mattered again. Serial numbers reentered logs. Equipment came wrapped not just in canvas, but in expectation.

Most of it was ordinary. That was the miracle.

Cots replaced damp ground. Blankets arrived that did not smell of salt or smoke. Tools appeared in quantities that allowed men to stop borrowing from tomorrow. Replacement uniforms did not erase the dirt, but they acknowledged it.

Water systems improved first. Pumps were installed properly. Lines ran where there once had been only buckets and arguments. The water buffaloes stopped standing alone as talismans and became part of something resembling infrastructure. Men washed when they could and learned to recognize the difference between clean enough and hopeful.

The losses of LST-599 were not forgotten. They were supplanted. Every crate unloaded from Guam carried the unspoken knowledge that it was standing in for something that had burned or sunk. No one said the ship's name out loud anymore. The supplies arrived without ceremony, without explanation, making good on a promise logistics never spoke of but always enforced.

The mess improved next. Coffee was no longer rationed to morale days. Food came hot more often than not. The pots acquired earlier—won in circumstances no one documented—were put to work properly now, boiling water in volume, feeding men who had learned to eat fast and standing. There were tents and field tables.

Maintenance followed. Spare parts filled gaps that improvisation could only bridge temporarily. Aircraft that had been kept aloft by stubbornness and ingenuity began receiving the attention they deserved. The tempo remained brutal, but it became sustainable. Morale responded cautiously.

Figure 52. Engine maintenance.

No one celebrated. No one trusted improvement enough to name it. But shoulders straightened slightly. Jokes returned—not many, and not loud. Men slept deeper when they slept at all.

The airfield remained under fire and the rain remained relentless. The work remained endless, but now it was possible to look ahead for more than twelve hours. Fred noticed the change, not in the reports, but in small things. Fewer arguments over tools. Fewer corners that were cut because there was nothing else to try. Fewer moments when survival alone dictated decisions.

The war did not ease. The squadron did not relax. The island loosened its grip just enough to allow function over desperation. In May, that was the difference between holding and breaking.

CHAPTER 43 – SHURI LINE

1–10 May 1945

In early May, VMF-322 flew almost exclusively in support of the effort to crack the Shuri Line—the Japanese defensive masterpiece stretching across the island's width. Below them, the war arranged itself into grinding sectors:

- 1st Marine Division assaulting Dakeshi and Wana

- 6th Marine Division bleeding against Sugar Loaf

- 77th Infantry Division grinding through the east.

- 7th and 96th Infantry Divisions forcing the central corridor.

There was no single front. Only pressure applied everywhere, constantly.

Figure 53. Marine does the Okinawa dash.

01 May 1945

Bad weather, minimal sorties.

02 May 1945

Bad weather, minimal sorties.

03 May 1945

Airfield construction continues, runway treacherous.

One alert was sounded at **1930**.

04 May 1945

They were scrambling before sunrise. The call came across Operations before anyone had finished coffee—urgent enough to erase fatigue without clearing it.

Radar plots came up fast: enemy aircraft inbound in numbers large enough to argue about and close enough not to. MAG-33 went airborne as a group.

Corsairs lifted wherever a runway still existed, climbing into a flaming sky already fractured by cloud and smoke. The engagement unfolded with a speed that felt unreal even as it happened. Enemy aircraft arrived in waves—and disappeared faster than they could reorganize.

In less than an hour they'd destroyed thirty enemy planes and damaged eleven more badly enough not to matter again. It would later be called **Turkey Shoot #2**, spoken without celebration and with more disbelief than pride. The burning sky had finally tipped— unmistakably. Again, VMF-323 carried the day. Their pilots accounted for twenty-four destroyed and ten damaged, flying with the aggression that had become signature and the discipline that kept losses from compounding.

But that wasn't what everyone talked about afterward.

1Lt. Jarvis

The call came from the fleet. A Judy had broken through, lining up on a destroyer already maneuvering hard, AA guns firing everything they had. Friendly anti-aircraft fire filled the air so completely it blurred the line between protection and hazard. **First Lieutenant Jarvis**, VMF-322, went after the Judy anyway.

Jarvis flew directly through the A.A> bullets. The Corsair shuddered under impacts—friendly bursts detonating close enough to bruise the cockpit air, enemy rounds tearing into metal with intent. Jarvis held the dive longer than was safe, longer than was wise, until the sight picture locked. He fired.

The Judy disintegrated two hundred yards off the destroyer's bow—close enough for debris to rain into the sea like punctuation. Jarvis pulled out trailing damage that should have ended the flight immediately. The cowling was torn open. The port wing shredded. The empennage chewed thin. The tail wheel barely hung where it belonged.

He brought it home anyway. When the Corsair rolled to a stop, it looked less like a fighter than a collection of parts that had agreed to remain airborne out of stubbornness alone. Ground crews stared longer than protocol encouraged. Fred didn't say anything. He didn't need to. The destroyer's captain recommended Jarvis for the Distinguished Flying Cross before the engine had finished ticking cool.

Figure 54. Unidentified damaged Corsair.

05 May 1945

The next day erased any suggestion that momentum meant relief.

Thirty-eight close air support strikes went out against the 32nd Japanese Regimental Headquarters—dumps, caves, command posts, gun emplacements buried so deep they had to be persuaded rather than destroyed. Aircraft flew low. They flew repeatedly. Results were logged as effective, which meant resistance shifted, and men on the ground could move again. It also meant aircraft returned shot through, damage added to the ledger without comment. One of them did not return.

\#

Major Arthur Turner, Executive Officer of VMF-323, was hit over enemy positions. Observers saw him bail out at roughly five hundred feet, his chute barely formed before he dropped into ground no one controlled long enough to claim. All front-line units were alerted. Search efforts began immediately—and stalled just as quickly. Nothing moved near those coordinates without drawing fire. The day ended with Turner's name still on the board.

Fred looked at it longer than protocol required. By nightfall, the weather was turning again. May had made its intentions clear.

The Corsairs flew thirteen, fourteen missions a day, covering infantry from all directions as the Japanese fell back into the rain-clogged southern peninsula. Fred watched tracers reaching upward through broken clouds as he lined up another strike.

CHAPTER 44 – ACCIDENTS WAITING TO HAPPEN

The first warnings came quietly. A VMF-322 pilot on final approach clipped the blade of a bulldozer parked too close to the runway edge—one of dozens carving Kadena into something resembling an airfield. The Corsair jolted sideways. A tire shredded. The right aileron tore free.

Instead of forcing the landing, the pilot did the only thing he could.

He poured on throttle and stayed in the air.

Fred reached the strip as the crippled Corsair staggered seaward, trailing fragments of its own skin. Two miles offshore, the pilot bailed out. His chute blossomed pale against the haze. A destroyer escort, USS St. George, plucked him from the water. The man survived. The lesson did not.

The runway was becoming as dangerous as the enemy.

Figure 55. Damaged Corsair on runway.

06 May 1945—Friendly Fire

The enemy big guns found the strip early. Shells landed close enough to scatter men still moving into position, punching holes through coral and steel matting alike. The runway shuddered. Fragments rattled across revetments and fuselages already scarred by weeks of abuse.

When the shelling lifted, six aircraft were damaged. No fire. No spectacle. Just more work added to a ledger that never cleared. Crews moved immediately, filling craters, dragging aircraft clear, deciding what could wait and what could not.

Flying resumed anyway. That morning, VMF-312 launched on a routine CAP north of the field. Visibility was uneven—sun glare low, cloud hanging in broken layers. Radio chatter stayed light.

Then one aircraft appeared where none should have been. **Second Lieutenant Karl,** VMF-312, sighted a plane breaking out of haze and made a split-second decision that would never be recalled. The silhouette fit expectation. The timing felt wrong. Training closed the gap between uncertainty and action. He attacked.

It was a Corsair belonging to **Major Ed Cameron**, VMF-322. Cameron saw the tracers before he understood them. He jettisoned what he could and pushed for the sea as control degraded. There was no time for radio argument—only the need to keep flying long enough to choose where it would stop. He ditched hard but upright. Rescue followed quickly.

Behind him, the mistake finished unfolding. Karl pulled too hard, too fast. His Corsair rolled, stalled, and disappeared north of Motobu—no correction, no recovery, no blame that mattered.

The board changed. No one said accident. No one said friendly fire.

By afternoon the strip reopened fully. CAP coverage was adjusted. Pilots launched with reminders they already knew—and would still forget when seconds ruled. Fred read the incident summary standing, paper already smeared with mud. Two aircraft lost. One pilot alive that shouldn't have been. One not. Air superiority had not made the war safer. It had only changed the ways men died. Okinawa wasn't just trying to kill them anymore. They were beginning to kill each other.

The enemy had attacked repeatedly all day, dropping bombs and strafing the runway.

Alerts sounded at **0210**, **0855**, **1240**, **2016**.

07 May 1945

It happened again. Two VMF-322 Corsairs returned low and fast—not from enemy pressure, but confusion. Tracers had crossed their flight paths where tracers should never have been. No hits. No ditching. Just the unmistakable realization that friendly guns had fired again.

The reports came clipped and careful:

"Couldn't get a clear ID."

"Silhouette matched."

"No markings visible through glare."

Fred didn't argue. The pattern was already visible, and patterns were what killed people.

That afternoon, Fred met with Axtell and Day. They met in a leaking operations hut that rattled whenever distant guns spoke. A map of southern Okinawa lay pinned to the table, edges curled, grid lines smudged by fingers tracing too many failures and too few victories.

"That makes two days," Fred said. Not accusation. Fact.

"Identification's breaking down," Day said.

Axtell leaned on the table. "Everyone's flying low. Weather's flattening altitudes. Silhouettes look identical through cloud and glare."

"Doesn't matter," Fred said. "We can't afford another mistake."

No one argued.

They changed procedures immediately. Adjusted CAP altitudes where weather allowed.

Mandatory IFF verification before engagement. Simplified radio challenges—short, unmistakable phrases. No freelancing. No assumptions.

"Anyone unsure breaks off," Fred said. "No heroics. No second guesses." They didn't pretend it would fix everything. Friendly fire wasn't born of stupidity or malice. It came from fatigue, identical aircraft, compressed timelines, and men forced to

decide in seconds with incomplete information. They could only reduce probability. When the meeting broke, Axtell paused at the door. "Could've been worse." Fred met his eyes. "Tomorrow is another day."

Alerts were sounded at **0015**, **0220**, **1925**, and **2020.**

Figure 55. Reloading of a Corsair.

08 May 1945

Clear weather allowed for normal flight operations. All squadrons took part in 123 CAP sorties, 12 night patrols, and 13 CAS sorties. enemy artillery, mortars and logistic targets.

Alerts were sounded at **1900, 1950, 2018, 2100, 2155**.

CHAPTER 45 – THE NICK ENGAGEMENT

10 May 1945

They were finishing a routine CAP. Four Corsairs from VMF-312 held station at ten thousand feet, engines steady, the sky clear enough to invite complacency.

Captain Ken Reusser led the division of 4 corsairs, with **First Lieutenant Robert Klingman** tucked tight on his wing. Nothing on the board suggested trouble. Nothing in the air hinted that history was preparing to intrude. Then Reusser saw it.

A thin vapor trace arcing high above them—too straight, too deliberate to be weather. Twenty-five thousand feet. Maybe higher. He keyed his radio and requested permission to investigate. Clearance came before the controller finished speaking. The four Corsairs climbed.

At twenty-eight thousand feet, cold began to bite into metal.

At thirty-two thousand, engines complained.

At thirty-six thousand, two aircraft peeled away— ceiling reached, performance collapsing, no disgrace in survival.

Reusser and Klingman kept climbing. The oxygen mask pressed cold against Klingman's face. Controls felt heavy, uncooperative. Above thirty-seven thousand feet, the sky darkened, thinned, hardened—the kind of sky where only a fool or a fighter pilot lingered.

Then the NICK appeared. Small. Fast. Silver-glinting. Cruising south with the confidence of altitude and distance, certain it could not be reached. Reusser checked his gauges and made the decision. "Lighten the ships." They fired short bursts—not at the enemy, but into empty sky—burning ammunition to shed weight, coaxing the last unwilling knots from engines already at the edge. The Corsairs clawed upward until the altimeters brushed 38,000 feet. They were on the NICK's tail.

Reusser cut inside its turn, forcing it north. He fired first—short, disciplined bursts walking across the left wing and engine cowling. Metal tore free in glittering fragments. It should have been decisive. The NICK held steady.

Klingman slid forward to finish it. He squeezed the trigger. Nothing. The cold had frozen his guns. There was no time to break off. No margin to wait. Klingman throttled forward and aimed the only weapon left. The propeller.

He struck the NICK's rudder cleanly. The impact shuddered through his aircraft like a blow to living bone. The enemy wobbled, corrected, staggered—but stayed airborne. Klingman broke away, circled, came back in. The second strike tore the rudder away and smashed into the right stabilizer.

The NICK dipped, tried to hold altitude. Klingman lined up again.

Figure 56. Bob Klingman

The third impact sheared off what remained of the stabilizer. This time the aircraft did not recover. It rolled once—steep and final—then dropped into cloud below. Finished.

The engagement had lasted for **one hour and forty-five minutes**. The pursuit covered **185** nautical miles.

Klingman's Corsair limped home riddled with damage—holes in the wing, cowling torn back, the propeller bent and scarred beyond reason. It should not have flown. It should not have climbed. It should not have survived the collision.

But it returned to Kadena. Men gathered around the aircraft in silence, studying the ruined propeller, the battered wing, the machine that had done something no manual had ever imagined.

Reusser and Klingman climbed down without flourish. Everyone on Okinawa understood what had happened that morning. It was not simply a kill. It was one of the most remarkable acts of aerial combat of the war.

Alerts were called at **0015**, **0220**, **1925**, and **2020**.

CHAPTER 46 – CHOCOLATE DROP HILL

11 May 1945

Turkey Shoot #3 took place. In less than two hours, fighters downed thirteen enemy planes, with honors going to two VMF-323 pilots, each of whom accounted for four enemy planes.

Alerts were sounded at **0100** and **0840**.

12 May 1945 Sugar Loaf

By the final week of April, the fight slid west toward terrain that refused abstraction—Sugar Loaf Hill, Horseshoe, Half-Moon. Ground that later in May shredded entire companies of the 6th Marine Division and made casualty figures feel dishonest.

The Marines signaled for air.

Fred flew his Corsairs low enough to see helmet colors below—green and brown shapes pressed flat against the slope, pinned by sniper fire and mortars buried deep into limestone that swallowed punishment and gave nothing back.

The Corsairs lined up their runs, rockets punching into the Horseshoe's rock face. Stone exploded outward. Dust and debris rained down over defenders long enough to matter.

It wasn't enough to take the hill. But it kept Marines from dying where they lay.

By Okinawa's measure, that counted.

Fred taxied after returning from the mission and shut down last. As he climbed down, the sun bled out behind the ridges they'd just left, the burning sky reddening not from fire but from the simple mechanics of evening.

12–16 May Dakeshi Ridge/ Chocolate Drop

Okinawa had taught everyone how resistance worked.

It did not rush. It did not announce itself.

It waited until momentum gathered, then pressed back just hard enough to stall it.

The next major resistance hardened along the Chocolate Drop Hill—a 130-foot beast of a dragon that guarded the approach to the Shuri Line, along with Flattop Hill. Dense limestone ridges sitting astride the road network feeding the Army's push south. Here, the Japanese did not contest ground for its own sake. They held the angles that mattered. Artillery nested on reverse slopes. Machine guns lived inside rock. Observation was done from places no tank could see and no bombardment could permanently erase.

For the 77th and 96th Infantry Divisions, the line was a choke point.

For VMF-322, it became routine.

13 May 1945 The Runaway Runway

Since 01 APR, Seabee crews worked around the clock. Floodlights stabbed the night. Bulldozers crawled the strip like metal insects. Craters appeared faster than they could be filled. A pilot returning from a successful sortie caught a raised lip of coral from a filled hole. The Corsair bucked, slammed sideways, and tore itself apart in sparks. The pilot walked away, shaken, the smell of burning rubber still in his hair. No one spoke. They understood.

Lost At Sea

Lt. Ralph Pinkerton's loss did not announce itself. No flash. No impact seen from the line. No crowd running toward fire. He just didn't come home. Just a Corsair that did not call in. A scheduled return that didn't become a silhouette on approach. One minute that turned into ten.

Operations asked the question in the careful language men used when they already knew the answer. "Any contact?" Controllers answered with static and uncertainty. "Anyone get a visual?"

Weather and sea blended until the horizon became theory. The burning sky over Okinawa was full of mistakes waiting to happen, and the water was always ready to accept whatever fell into it. A search grid went up. Dumbo aircraft circled. A destroyer changed course, wakes cutting new chalk lines across gray water. But the sea did not offer wreckage. It rarely did.

Fred's board read overdue, then MIA. The MIA sat there longer than anyone wanted. Men would glance at it as they passed, as if looking hard enough might pull the pilot back out of the Pacific like a stubborn hook. It didn't.

Eventually the label changed, not because anyone found him, but because time makes decisions when men cannot.

13 May 1945—Lt Ralph Pinkerton—KIA — lost at sea—aircraft destroyed

The board did not show the thing that haunted them: the idea of a man in water, waiting, watching the sky, listening for engines that never came. That kind of death didn't leave scorch marks.

It left a quiet in the squadron that lasted longer than smoke.

Also lost: **Lt. Murray** of VMF-323. Went down in flames from enemy antiaircraft fire. **Cpt. Arndt,** of VMF(N) 543 also failed to return to base. He was last seen dropping flares eight miles northeast.

The VAL Take Down

The Val came in low, steady, committed. There was no evasion in its approach, no attempt to disguise intent.

It flew directly at the destroyer below, already throwing its bow hard over, guns lifting instinctively toward a threat that once committed would allow no correction.

First Lieutenant F. B. Warren, VMF-322, spotted it immediately.

He rolled in from altitude without waiting for clearance, shoving the Corsair into a dive that carried him straight into the rising curtain of friendly fire. Forty-millimeter bursts climbed toward the Val in measured arcs, filling the burning sky between ship and aircraft with metal that did not distinguish between targets. Warren ignored it.

He closed the distance hard, pushing inside every safe margin, the destroyer swelling beneath the Val until separation became academic. Five hundred yards. That was when the shell hit.

A 40mm round tore through Warren's right wing, shredding the aileron and snapping control authority in an instant. The Corsair rolled unevenly, response distorted, surfaces no longer answering clean command.

Below him, the Val disintegrated and struck the sea short of the destroyer. Its attack was finished.

Warren tested what control remained—seconds that felt deliberate, careful, unhurried despite the violence. It wasn't enough.

The aircraft wandered despite every correction. He turned toward shore. At fifty yards offshore, in four feet of water, Warren bailed out cleanly, hitting the surf hard but upright. The Corsair continued without him, skidded forward, then collapsed into itself.

Men from a nearby shore battery reached him almost immediately, hauling him clear before shock or injury could take hold. He walked back under his own power—soaked, shaken, alive.

The destroyer remained afloat. The board reflected another enemy aircraft destroyed. Another Corsair lost. In

May, victories were measured not in numbers—but in margins.

Alerts called out at **0205** and **1845**.

14 May 1945—A Second Warning

The island was setting conditions. By mid-May, the runway had stopped forgiving even small mistakes. Telegraphing its punch. Another landing. Another hazard. Another Corsair lost.

This time the pilot taxied off the strip and sank into a soft patch of coral dust. The gear collapsed. The aircraft snapped forward, propeller shearing clean as the nose struck.

Again, the pilot lived. Again, the loss was logged as operational.

But Fred felt something tightening across the field—a silent countdown. That night, the new procedures went live. Pilots adjusted. Controllers sharpened calls. Everyone flew colder, tighter.

The burning sky did not become safer. But the pilots refocused. In the May burning sky, discipline was all that stood between accidents and safety.

Kakai Shima

The first daylight strike on Kakai Shima launched with sixteen aircraft from VMF-312.

Each carried a single 500-pound bomb and a full complement of rockets. The formation descended through scattered clouds toward the enemy airfield—still operational, still defiant.

They released on schedule. Sixteen bombs fell clean. One hundred twenty-three rockets followed, tearing across revetments and runway surfaces in disciplined, deliberate runs.

Figure 58. VMF-312 flightline.

Enemy anti-aircraft fire rose immediately—light, medium, heavy—layered and accurate. Not overwhelming. Precise. Bursting at dive paths, pull-out points, and turn radii.

Major Richard M. "Dick" Day, commanding officer of VMF-312, held his line. He was last seen in a controlled dive, flying clean through the pattern as heavy AA detonated close enough to lift his Corsair in flashes of black and white. No abrupt deviation. No distress call. Moments later, a large ball of fire rose from the target area. No parachute followed.

The strike withdrew and passed coordinates to Air-Sea Rescue. Dumbo aircraft searched in widening arcs. No wreckage. No raft. No signal. By noon, the conclusion was unavoidable.

VMF-312 "**Day's Knights**," had lost their skipper.

Alerts sounded at **0300** and **1910**.

A Moment of Silence

The report reached Kadena before the smoke over Kakai Shima had risen. Fred read it once. Then again. There was no ambiguity to resolve. Day hadn't missed a rendezvous. He hadn't drifted beyond a search grid. He was simply gone.

Axtell arrived first, coral dust streaking his sleeve. He didn't sit. He didn't speak. He stood in the doorway until Fred looked up.

"He held the dive," Fred said.

Axtell nodded. He already knew.

Mathis arrived moments later, closing the door behind him out of habit. The noise of the field pressed against the canvas—engines, machinery and distant guns, but inside the room the air held still.

"He taught half the pilots on this island," Axtell said quietly.

"Maybe more." Fred rested his hands on the map table, tracing terrain lines he'd memorized long before May began. "He knew the risks."

"That doesn't help," Mathis said.

"No," Fred replied. "It doesn't."

There was no checklist for this part. Just absence. "We'll help cover their tasking," Fred said after a moment.

"They've got a great one in **Major Hugh I. Russell.** We all know that.".

"J. R., give Hugh anything we can until they sort things out."

Axtell nodded. No one mentioned memorials. No one spoke of the next strike.

When they left, Fred remained alone briefly, listening to the field—the same field that had taken more men than the enemy in the last week alone.

MAG-33—Command Presence

The command meeting convened under canvas. **Colonel Ward E. Dickey**, commander of MAG-33, waited until all representatives were present before speaking. "Gentlemen, we lost Major Richard Day this morning." No elaboration followed.

"VMF-312 remains operational. A temporary command arrangement will be announced. Tasking will not pause." He let that settle. "We operate as a group—not as isolated squadrons. Fighters, night fighters, torpedo bombers, service and headquarters elements. The enemy doesn't differentiate. Neither will we."

No one argued. "No forward memorials until operational conditions allow," Dickey continued. "Major Day's service will be recognized properly."

Then, quieter: "This does not diminish the loss."

The meeting broke without ceremony. Outside, engines cycled. Construction crews worked in standing water. The war did not acknowledge grief. MAG-33 had just absorbed another name into its accounting.

Everyone there understood the balance sheet was still open.

CHAPTER 47 – THE LAST RETURN

16 May 1945—Shuri

The day began like all the others on Okinawa—too early, too wet, too loud.

At **0305**, the strip was rocked by five bombs that dropped in the Radio-Radar area, behind the Control Tower. Moderate equipment damage and two marines were evacuated.

Rain swept across Kadena in slow silver sheets, blurring the ridgelines to the south. Mortar thumps rolled up the valley like distant doors slamming shut. Engineers were already on the strip, filling the previous night's craters, dragging aside coral debris, repositioning floodlights yet again. This was the sixth straight day the airfield had been barely serviceable.

Barely was good enough. VMF-322 had the first launch window.

\#

Mathis stepped into Operations with the same loose, easy gait he had carried since Cherry Point. He smelled of machine oil and damp canvas, his flight suit already streaked with coral dust. He tapped the mission board lightly with two fingers. They flew everything that would lift.

By dawn, six CAPs were already rotating overhead—twenty sorties stitched into the orange sky in overlapping arcs meant to keep the enemy down long enough for the ground war to breathe. Engines cycled without pause. Crews barely finished turning one aircraft before another pilot climbed in. There would be no margin today.

"CAS south," he said. "Sugar Loaf." Fred looked up. "They're pinned again?"

Mathis nodded once, already reading the board the way he always did—quick, calm, taking the bad news like it belonged to him personally.

"Fifth Marines. Reverse-slope guns chewing the approaches. They can't move. They can't pull back. They can only hold until we buy them a breath." Fred watched him sign the roster—quick loops, confident strokes. Routine. Comforting.

Dangerous.

"Be careful down there," Fred said quietly.

Mathis smirked. "Always am."

"That's not what I said." Mathis paused and met his eyes. The grin softened into something more honest. "I know," he said. "I'll bring them home."

Then he was gone, helmet under one arm, walking toward the line of Corsairs waiting in rain and mist. Engineers paused to let him pass. A few Marines nodded. Everyone on the island knew J.R. Mathis—knew his steadiness, his humor, his clarity under pressure. Some pilots flew like they were tempting fate. Mathis flew like they were on a first name basis.

The Strike—Sugar Loaf/ Horseshoe / Half Moon

Since the 12th of May, the marines of the 22nd Marine regiment had been fighting to survive. Before noon the CAS strike of sixteen Corsairs, loaded heavy, pressed low by weather and urgency. The request had come from the south where the fight had settled into mud and blood below the Sugar Loaf–Horseshoe–Half Moon complex— three mutually supporting hilltops, produced the most vicious ground action on the island.

Inside those positions was an entire regiment, all connected by reinforced tunnels. Interlocking fields of fire from each hill protected the slopes and approaches of the others. Enemy artillery supported all of Sugar Loaf's terrain. Machine gun positions lined Half-Moon and Horseshoe, while Sugar Loaf, was filled with concrete reverse slope positions that would have to be eliminated one by one—by hand.

Units of the 6th Marines were pinned—dug into shallow depressions while fire from Japanese reverse-slope positions raked every approach. The infantry could not move. They could not withdraw. They could only hold. The help was airborne.

Mathis flew on the strike lead's wing. What was left of Sugar Loaf was already burning. Wrecked tanks clawing uselessly at slopes. Marines of the 6th and Army's 96th Infantry Divisions lay pinned along the ravine floor, machine-gun fire stitching from caves cut deep into limestone.

"Red Leader on station," Mathis said calmly. The FAC's voice crackled. *"White phosphorus marks. Left ridge shoulder. Clear that or we don't move. "Copy," Mathis replied. "Rolling in." The ridge answered first.*

Figure 59. Corsair rocket attack.

They came down the ridgeline low enough to feel
the heat rising off burning positions. Rockets cracked
against concealed gun pits that had already chewed
through two platoons. Strafing runs shredded machine-
gun nests firing diagonally across the Marines' left flank.
Tracers climbed in furious arcs, thick enough to feel solid.
Mathis trimmed slightly, held his dive. At eighteen
hundred feet he loosed the rockets—white fire punching
into a cave mouth. His wingmen followed with 500-
pounders. Stone, fire, and dirt erupted.

Below, Marines surged forward—only yards, but
yards they could not have taken before.

"Second run," Mathis said. *"Spacing tight. They're
awake now."* They dove again. This time the fire was
heavier. Organized. Interlocking. A Corsair behind him
took a hit but stayed airborne.

On the third pass, smoke finally shifted, and
forward observers signaled movement—measured not in
yards, but in the fact that men could lift their heads
without being killed for it.

"Good effect!" the FAC called. *"Left bunker
neutralized. Advancing!"* It was, by every measure, an ass-
saving mission. It kept the line from folding. It kept
Marines alive.

Mathis pulled up through smoke, heart pounding.
He glanced down—tiny figures crawling forward,
surviving. He loved this work. Not the killing.

The role of savior.

By early afternoon, the Corsairs returned in
fractions. Some limped in low. Some came back early.
Some carried more damage than they deserved; others
carried less than they'd earned. The field stayed open by
persistence rather than design—steel matting ending
abruptly, coral fill shifting under weight, rain trapped
everywhere it could collect.

Fred stood near Operations as aircraft began to return. He watched them the way commanders do—not as machines, but as men he knew by the way they approached, by the engine note, by their shadow on the coral. He could identify pilots before they called in, before wheels touched ground.

The light was bad. Floodlights burned too bright against gathering haze, flattening depth and blinding eyes that had spent hours adjusting to smoke and cloud. The runway shimmered, angles wrong, distances deceptive.

Mathis came in steady. Too steady. Fred felt it before he understood it. The glide path marginally off. The Corsair touched down and bounced. The second impact came harder—gear biting unevenly into a surface that wasn't finished. The aircraft slewed left, wingtip striking metal, then earth. Momentum carried it forward until it finally stopped.

Fred was already moving. Crewmen ran. Medics followed. Someone shouted for equipment that arrived too late to matter. Mathis never left the cockpit.

There was no dramatic explosion—only the sound of bent metal settling into silence under floodlights that kept shining as if nothing had changed.

Fred reached the edge of the cordon and stopped. This one was not ambiguous. This one did not allow hope.

Later, the day's numbers would go on the board: Six CAPs flown. Twenty sorties.

One CAS strike. Sixteen aircraft. Sugar Loaf held. Sixth Marines still in the fight.

None of it would say the most dangerous part of the CAS mission came after the guns were silent. None of it would say the hill named Sugar Loaf would cost the 6th Marine Division over 3,000 men.

Fred stood there until someone touched his arm. He nodded once.

He turned back toward Operations. The war did not slow. Something essential had shifted.

For the first time since Okinawa began, Fred Rauschenbach felt the weight of command settle somewhere it would not lift again.

An Empty Hole

They gathered where they always gathered—standing, helmets hooked under arms, flight suits streaked with oil and coral dust. No one needed to be told why.

Fred stood in front of them.

"**Major J.R. Mathis** was lost today," he said.

He didn't raise his voice. He didn't lower it either. The words landed because they were precise.

"He flew CAS in support of the 5th Marines at Sugar Loaf Hill. The mission succeeded. The ground units held." No one moved.

"Major Mathis completed his runs and returned with the others. He was lost on landing due to runway conditions and glare." He let it sit—not because it needed explanation, but because it required acknowledgment.

"He was my executive officer," Fred continued. "He was also a pilot who flew clean, led correctly, and never wasted a man's confidence. He did his job today exactly the way he always did it."

A pause. "He was my friend."

"The squadron will continue flying. Tasking remains unchanged. Command continuity is in place. Major Maas will assume duties as X.O." Somewhere behind them an engine turned over—the war, indifferent.

"For those of you who flew with him today—thank you. For those of you who didn't—you'll fly tomorrow." He nodded once. "That's all."

They held position a moment longer, then dispersed without sound.

The Toast

Night came without ceremony. Fred returned to his quarters long after the strip quieted, after the generators settled into their endless hum. He closed the door and sat without turning on the light.

From the footlocker at the end of the cot, he took out the bottle. It was half gone.

He turned it once in his hand, remembering the night Mathis had brought it back from a supply run that had produced answers no one asked for. Remembering Mathis's grin when he'd said we scored. Fred poured two fingers into a chipped tin cup. He didn't stand. There was no one to perform for. He raised the cup slightly—not high, not ceremonial.

"To you, J.R.," he said quietly. No rank. No flourish. Just truth. He drank.

The whiskey burned harsh and familiar. He poured a second measure and let it sit untouched.

Then he took the untouched cup outside and tipped it gently onto the earth. The soil absorbed it without comment.

"Brother," he said. He went back inside. Tomorrow would come.

\#

Fred heard the footsteps before he saw the figure emerging from the dim line of tents—slow, deliberate, carrying the weight of a man who'd already lived too many evenings like this one. Axtell stopped a few feet away, hands in his pockets, looking toward the runway where Mathis and his Corsair had ceased to exist. Fred stepped out, joined him. Neither man spoke at first.

They were both commanders. They had each learned silence was often safer than words.

They had both experienced loss and grief.

The rain had eased, leaving the night strangely clear. Floodlights cast hard bars across the strip. In the distance, crews moved like slow shadows working in exhausted rhythm. Axtell's gaze dropped to the bottle near Fred's boot.

"J.R. would've appreciated that."

"He would've fought me for it," Fred said.

"Only if he thought he'd win."

Fred let out a thin breath that almost qualified as a laugh. "He usually did."

"I'm sorry, Fred," Axtell said. The words were simple. They felt earned.

Fred nodded once. "I know. First you lost TURNER, then we lost DAY, now I lose J.R."

Axtell didn't smile. "He was one of the good ones."

"They're all good ones," Fred said.

"Yes," Axtell replied, quiet and honest. "But some more than others."

Axtell watched the floodlights for a moment, eyes dark with fatigue. "Your men will look at your face tomorrow before they look at the burning sky," he said. "They'll fly because you pretend it doesn't hurt. They'll fight because you act like you're not bleeding inside."

Fred swallowed. "It doesn't feel like strength. It feels like a façade."

"That's all it ever feels like," Axtell said. "We've been pretending since the first man died under our command. If my hands shake, the whole squadron shakes with me."

Fred didn't answer. He reached for another cup, poured whiskey for them both.

Axtell rested his hand briefly on his shoulder—just enough pressure to anchor, not comfort.

"You're not alone in this," he said. "Not tonight. Not tomorrow. Not at Wana or Sugar Loaf or whatever fresh hell comes next." He took his hand back. They raised their cups in a silent toast.

They stood together for another stretch of silence, watching the lights flicker across the airfield—bright, blinding, uncaring.

When Axtell finally stepped away, he paused just long enough to say, "We lead from the front. Mathis knew that. That's why he flew for you." Then he vanished back into the tents.

Fred remained where he was, the weight of command settling around him like another layer of damp air. He looked at the strip, then at the sky—dark, vast, indifferent.

Tomorrow he would stand in front of his men. Tomorrow he would be the spine.

Tonight, he allowed himself one breath that trembled. Then he swallowed it down.

He turned back toward his Command tent.

Alerts sounded at **2007, 2143, 2255**.

CHAPTER 48 – WANA RIDGE /WANA DRAW

17 May 1945

Major J.B. Maas assumed duties as Executive Officer of VMF-322. There was no ceremony. No speech. Maas arrived already briefed, already aware of what he was stepping into. He met Fred early, reviewed tasks, walked the line once, and began doing the work as if it had always been his. The squadron adjusted because it had to. Names changed on the board. Responsibilities shifted. The fight continued.

At **0710**, a huge fire erupted on the taxiway, when a napalm tank fell off one plane and was struck by the VMF-312 plane following immediately behind in line. Shortly after, five rockets ignited and shot through the encampment. No injuries or damage was caused, but the plane was destroyed.

Five alerts were sounded at **0014**, **0205**, **0745**, **2010**, and **2107**.

18 May 1945

Four VMF-322 planes spotted a surfaced enemy submarine at 0840. They dove from 10,000 feet, strafed the entire length of the submarine. Smoke, debris, and an oil slick were observed after the craft submerged. One Corsair failed over the water—engine trouble, abrupt and unrecoverable. The pilot made the correct calls, jettisoned what he could, and bailed out clean. Recovery boats reached him in time. He returned soaked, shaken, and alive—a reminder that procedure still mattered when luck held. The reprieve did not last.

Alerts were sounded at **0130**, **0425**, **1920**, **2155**.

19 May 1945

Another aircraft went into the sea. Weather had turned again—low ceiling, uneven visibility, wind cutting across approach paths without warning. The pilot never transmitted distress. Those who watched from altitude saw only a brief uncontrolled descent before the aircraft disappeared into gray water. **Lt. George E. Allen** of VMF-322 crashed into the sea attempting to get through the overcast. Search efforts began immediately. By mid-day, the conclusion hardened into record: pilot killed, cause attributed to weather. No wreckage recovered. No counterargument possible. Fred updated the Board without comment.

His body was recovered two days later.

Two alerts were called at **0235** and **0355**.

20 May 1945

The squadron began relocating its bivouac area to the north side of the airfield.

The move came out of necessity rather than comfort. Enemy fire had begun ranging closer at night. Construction patterns shifted again. Operations demanded different adjacency. Men packed what little they owned and carried it across mud that had learned their weight too well.

Tents went up where the ground allowed. Tools reappeared where they were needed most. The squadron rebuilt itself in place, as it had learned to do, in the pouring rain.

Fred watched the movement from Operations as aircraft cycled in and out. New XO.

Two aircraft lost. One pilot alive. One dead. Living quarters displaced again. None of it slowed the mission schedule. But the days had begun to stack. Okinawa had made its point clear: even survival now came one loss at a time.

Two alerts were called at **1833** and **1916**.

22 May 1945

The alerts rarely came from the air any more.

CAPs rotated overhead as scheduled, engines droning through layers of gray that offered little to hunt and less to surprise. Enemy aircraft showed themselves just often enough to justify vigilance and no more. Intercepts were brief. Contacts fleeting. Most flights returned having fired nothing at all. The burning sky was quiet.

The ground was not. Dakeshi Ridge had finally been taken by the 7th Marine Regiment on the 12th of May. Ahead lay the Wana Ridge and Wana Draw terrain. Just 1200 yards in front lay the next two objectives. Estimated to take perhaps one day to seize. It would take the 1st Marine Division for 18 days. It would cost 200 Marines for every 100 yards.

Every call that mattered now came from below— from forward observers embedded with 1st Marine Division, radios pressed close, voices measured and urgent. Wana Draw had become the narrowest part of the advance, where elements of the 5th Marines and 7th Marines were funneled into a terrain feature that favored the defender completely. What looked like a natural ravine on the map functioned as a deliberate kill zone. Targets were everywhere.

Gun ports opened from slopes that appeared empty until they fired. Mortar positions shifted just enough to stay alive. Cave mouths reappeared minutes after being hit, as though the ridge itself resisted

clearance. Japanese defenders of the 32nd Army—
primarily elements of the 62nd Division— fought from
reverse slopes and underground positions that could not
be neutralized, only suppressed.

CAS was no longer about finding the enemy. It was
about finding them at exactly the right moment. Aircraft
launched without pause, briefed enroute, redirected mid-
flight. Strike plans dissolved as quickly as they formed.
Smoke markers bloomed and vanished under rain and
wind. Grid references tightened—then tightened again—
until danger-close meant the difference between
movement and disaster. Pilots learned restraint where
aggression once ruled. They orbited longer. They waited
when they were told to wait. They dove in only when the
call came, not when impatience tempted.

Figure 60. Corsair landing.

At Wana Draw, a strike delivered too early
achieved nothing. A run delivered five minutes late killed
Marines who had already committed, believing support
was inbound.

Fred understood that with uncomfortable clarity.
He watched the board as requests stacked and fell away—
support for 5th Marines pinned low, then a sudden shift
east as 7th Marines attempted to widen the draw. To the
east, pressure from 7th Infantry Division around Conical

Hill helped fix Japanese units in place, but it did nothing to relieve the fire pouring into the ravines.

One flight arriving at the right second could turn a stalled assault into movement. One arriving even slightly wrong—wrong slope, wrong pocket, wrong timing— might as well not have flown.

The Corsair was still lethal. But lethality no longer decided the day. Influence did.

Influence at Wana Draw lasted only minutes at a time.

Fred marked the area differently, not with sortie counts or enemy strength, but with reminders written small in the corner of the board:

Timing.

Restraint.

Precision.

It wasn't glory that mattered here. It was relevance. At Wana Draw, relevance expired fast.

Wana Draw

Fred flew the lead. He hadn't planned to. The sortie roster hadn't demanded it. But the calls coming in from 5th Marines, 1st Marine Division, carried the particular edge that told him timing would decide everything. Not volume. Not courage. Timing.

The Corsairs climbed low and slowly into a ceiling that refused altitude. Cloud pressed them flat, forcing the formation into the narrow layer where flak lived. The air felt heavy, engines laboring as if they shared the pilots' fatigue.

"322 Lead to FAC," Fred said. *"On station."*

The reply came instantly, clipped and precise. *"Draw is hot. Marines pinned. Reverse slope fire. Stand by."* Fred rolled his shoulders once inside the cockpit and settled the nose.

Below them, Wana Draw opened like a wound— mud, shattered vegetation, shadowed slopes that looked empty until they killed people. Enemy contact in the air was irrelevant.

Everything that mattered was down there.

Smoke bloomed suddenly near the base of the draw, then tore apart in wind and rain. Fred adjusted immediately, recalculating without thinking, shifting the pattern so his wingmen could see what he could not. He led them down. The Corsair shuddered as he pushed through turbulence and sporadic bursts that rose late and inaccurate—the enemy gambling rather than aiming. Fred lined up on a fold of terrain the FAC had marked seconds earlier—one of those places that looked harmless until it erupted.

"Rockets." The release was clean.

White streaks vanished into shadow. The earth kicked upward violently, smoke and debris filling the draw just long enough for something important to change. *"Good hits,"* the FAC called. *"Movement on the left. They're moving. Stand by."*

Fred held orbit—tight, patient—resisting the urge to go back in. He knew better now. A second run without coordination was how Marines died.

Below, men rose from cover and advanced—not confidently, but possible.

That was all CAS ever really gave them.

The enemy tried to answer. Mortars coughed. Small arms flashed uselessly skyward. Fred shifted again, calling his wingmen through shallow dives that discouraged attention without inviting commitment.

Then the call came. *"That's it. We're through."* Fred acknowledged and pulled them away.

They climbed back into clouds, engines steady, aircraft unmarred this time, not because luck favored them, but because discipline had.

On the return leg, Fred said nothing. There was no room for reflection up there. No space to think about who used to sit on his wing—or who should still be alive. Flying demanded presence.

Grief waited for the ground.

As Kadena appeared beneath thinning haze, floodlights already burning for another night of unfinished construction, Fred felt the familiar tightening in his chest—not fear. Calculation.

Landing was still the most dangerous part.

He brought the Corsair in carefully, wheels touching down firm and deliberate, refusing the bounce that had taken Mathis. When the aircraft rolled to a stop, he cut power and sat a moment longer than usual. Fred climbed down and handed the aircraft off without comment, already turning back toward Operations.

Somewhere south of him, 5th Marines were moving again inside Wana Draw because VMF-322 had arrived at the right moment. Tomorrow, someone else will need the same thing.

There were three alerts at **0957**, **1950**, and **2300**.

24 May 1945

At 0530, an alert scrambled 38 fighters to meet an enemy attack. Thirty-two enemy planes were destroyed, with two additional that were probable, and seven damaged. **Captain H.J Valentine** of VMF-312 led a division of four planes into the melee, destroying thirteen enemy planes. **Lt. W. Farrell** of VMF-312 destroyed three planes, and damaged 2. **Lt. J.E Webster** of VMF-322 destroyed three Tojos and damaged one other.

One additional alert was called at **0800**.

28 May 1945

Days of poor weather hampered operations. A Red Alert was issued at 0215 to all units to prepare for another airborne attack. At 0316, one enemy plane succeeded in evading anti-aircraft fires and dropped five 100-pound bombs on the runway. **Two Marines were killed.**

Two additional alerts were sounded at **0750** and **2250**.

30 May 1945

As the month ended, **2Lt. R.D. Baker** of VMF-322 crashed into the sea while returning from patrol. Cause unknown, but extremely thick weather. Rescue efforts were unsuccessful.

During the final days of May, with the Japanese withdrawing from Shuri Castle, VMF-322 flew CAS almost continuously for the 7th ID, 96th ID, and 1st Marine Division as they advanced southward into melting terrain and collapsing defensive tunnels.

One CAS run struck artillery harassing the 31st Infantry Regiment; another helped the 5th Marines secure the last ridgeline overlooking the castle ruins. Each pass was met with sporadic but furious anti-aircraft fire. The war, though turning toward its end, had never felt farther from being done.

There were three alerts at **0957, 1950, 2300.**

CHAPTER 49 – FAREWELL

30 May 1945 Kadena VMF-322 CP

Fred received notification of reassignment orders just after sunrise, when the air still held a trace of coolness and the dust had yet to rise from the first vehicle passing along the perimeter road. VMF322 was being handed over to a new commander.

He crossed the airfield to VMF-323 operations tent and tracked down Axtell. "AX, I don't believe it, I've got Change of Command orders".

Axtell motioned for Fred to follow him, and the two men stepped outside.

"My replacement is flying in tomorrow, with the effective date of the orders tomorrow." Axtell shook his head slowly then said, "Well NY, you are not alone. I received my orders transmitted today also. But I've got two more weeks here, I'm not leaving until 16th of June." "They have me on a transport arriving in Guam on the June 2nd. No clue what my next destination is," grumbled Fred.

Axtell and Fred walked slowly together, comparing notes, memories, promises kept and promises broken. Two warriors, two aviators, two commanders of men. Their bond forged in service to each other, the nation and most importantly . . . to the men they led. They stopped at the end of the runway and watched as a flight returned. Turning to face each other, they shook hands, saluted one another. Each then executed an about-face and returned to their squadron.

31 May 1945

Fred had VMF-322 assembled in a tight formation on the coral strip, their faces steady, their bearing precise. Fred stood at the front, his uniform immaculate despite the weeks of mud and cordite that clung to everything on Okinawa. Beside him, Major Walter F. Lischeid waited calmly, hands behind his back, eyes taking in the squadron he was about to lead.

Fred addressed the squadron. "The fight goes on, and so will you. **Major Lischeid** takes over today, and you will give him the same professionalism, the same precision, the same grit you've shown under me." A faint breeze carried coral dust across the line. No one shifted.

"You know your duty," Fred continued. "You know the standard. Keep it. Raise it. And keep each other in the air."

When the adjutant finished reading the transfer of command, Lischeid stepped forward and saluted Fred with crisp formality. Fred returned it without hesitation—clean, sharp, without a hint of the weight inside him. Lischeid lowered his hand. Just the acknowledgment of a commander stepping forward into responsibility. Fred nodded once, approving the tone.

When the formation was dismissed, Fred stood there one moment longer, quiet, composed. He then turned and walked toward Operations to begin whatever came next. He had given VMF-322 everything. Now it was Major Lischeid's turn to carry them forward.

During April and May 1945, MAG-33 flew nearly 4,700 sorties over Okinawa—more than a thousand combat air patrols and over 600 close air support sorties. VMF-322 flew its share, and then some. None of it was decisive alone. Together, it kept the ground war moving.

Operational Summary—MAG-33 / Okinawa Campaign
(April–May 1945)

Squadron	April Sorties	May Sorties	Total
VMF-312	498	948	1,446
VMF-322	513	974	1,487
VMF-323	814	950	1,764
TOTAL	1,825	2,872	4,697

EPILOGUE

After Fred left VMF-322, the war continued without pause. Squadrons rotated. Names were replaced. Airfields moved. The machinery of victory ground forward, indifferent to who had stood in which place at which moment. That, too, had been part of the lesson. Fred learned that command is temporary, no matter how full or empty it feels at the time and that survival carries no obligation to justify itself.

All the men Fred trained, flew, and arrived with had already left the theater, except one. Most men he served with did not remain together after the war. A few names returned from time to time—in correspondence, in chance meetings in a HQ's hallway, in lists that confirmed what he already knew. Others did not return at all.

He had done the work that was asked of him, under conditions that allowed no margin and offered no quarter. He had led men until there were no familiar faces left to lead. He had watched a squadron become something entirely different and then entrusted it to the next hand.

He had commanded a moment. The squadron had carried the war.

VMF-322 entered Okinawa already diminished. Its supplies burned aboard LST-599 before the squadron ever touched land. Days later, the flight line took its own men lost not to the enemy, but to the ground beneath their feet. What followed was not recovery, but a slug fest.

Alongside the other squadrons of MAG-33, they held the burning sky—not as heroes, not as legends, but as a group of boys trained, scattered, and shaped by it, who carried the war forward together when nothing else was certain.

Frederick Martine Rauschenbach Remained in the Marine Corps after World War II, earning aeronautical engineering degrees from Annapolis and MIT, and contributing to the development of military ballistic and guided missile systems. He flew combat again in Korea, and served as executive officer of VMF-321, before leaving active duty in 1955. He is buried at Riverside National Cemetery.

Hugh Irving Russell Served with distinction as executive officer of VMF-312 and later commanded VMF-471. He left active Marine service in December 1946 and died in 1988.

George Axtell Jr. Continued his Marine Corps career after Okinawa, flying combat in Korea and later serving in Vietnam. He retired as a lieutenant general in 1974 and is buried at Arlington National Cemetery.

Quinton Roy Johns Served as executive officer and commanding officer in multiple Marine fighter squadrons. Promoted to lieutenant colonel in 1951, he was killed in an aviation accident later that year while on active duty.

Richard Maurice Day Commanding officer of VMF-312 during Operation Iceberg. He was killed in action on Okinawa on 14 May 1945.

Charlton Bidwell Ivey Sr Served in multiple headquarters and service squadrons as a staff officer and commander. He left active Marine service in 1946 and died in 2013.

Douglas Beebe Lenardson Served as operations officer and commanding officer in Marine observation and photographic squadrons during and after World War II. He retired due to deafness in 1951 and is buried at Fort Rosecrans National Cemetery.

Gregory "Pappy" Boyington After service with the Flying Tigers, rejoined the Marine Corps and earned both the Navy Cross and the Medal of Honor. He commanded multiple Marine fighter squadrons and retired as a colonel in 1947. He is buried at Arlington National Cemetery.

Jack Robinson "JR" Mathis Served as executive officer of VMF-322 during Operation Iceberg. He was killed in action on Okinawa on 17 May 1945.

Edmund Fryer Overend commanded multiple Marine fighter squadrons in the Pacific following his service in the "Flying Tigers". After the war, he earned advanced degrees, served in the Foreign Service and the United Nations. He died in 1971.

Figure 61. VMF-322 Officers, February 1945.

AUTHOR'S HISTORICAL NOTE

The events and characters depicted in **BOYS OF THE BURNING SKY** are grounded in historical record, squadron war diaries, after-action reports, and personal accounts from the Okinawa campaign of 1945. It is estimated that since 1912, there have been between 40,000-60,000 USMC aviators. The American Fighter Aces Association has the current count of USMC Aces standing at 122. That equates to a historical chance of 0.244% of making Ace if we use 50,000. 5 kills to be an Ace. There is no such list or category for CAS pilot achievement. Perhaps there should be.

Marine Fighter Squadron 322 (VMF-322), along with its sister squadrons in Marine Aircraft Group 33, flew hundreds of sorties in support of U.S. Army and Marine ground forces during one of the most destructive battles of the Pacific War.

While dates, places, and operations are drawn from history, the interior lives of the men—what they feared, carried, suffered, shared and withheld —are rendered with dramatic interpretation. The losses described were real. The conditions were real. The endurance required was real. Nothing in this account exceeds what was endured by those who lived it.

1. OPERATION ICEBERG and OKINAWA (1APRIL–22JUNE 1945). The Battle of Okinawa was the largest amphibious assault of the Pacific War and the final major campaign before the planned invasion of Japan. The Japanese 32nd Army under General Mitsuru Ushijima abandoned beach defense in favor of deeply layered, reverse slope positions anchored along the Shuri Line, a fortified belt of ridges, caves, and underground command posts running east–west across southern Okinawa. By mid-April, the battle had evolved into a war of attrition. Japanese forces avoided decisive engagement, instead

imposing steady casualties through artillery, mortars, and concealed machine-gun positions. Weather, terrain, and exhaustion increasingly shaped outcomes more than maneuver. Marine and Army aviation operating from Kadena and Yontan Airfields became essential to ground progress once naval gunfire and artillery proved insufficient to neutralize reverse-slope defenses. Both commanding generals died in the battle.

2. MARINE AIRCRAFT GROUP 33 (MAG-33)

Marine Aircraft Group 33 (MAG-33) operated as one of the principal Marine aviation elements supporting the Okinawa campaign. During April– May 1945, MAG-33 included:

- VMF-312

- VMF-322

- VMF-323

- VMF(N)-543 (night fighters)

- VMTB-232 (torpedo bombers)

- Supporting Headquarters and Service Squadrons

MAG-33 operated from escort carriers and later from land-based airfields under continuous shelling, flooding, and active construction. In addition to fighter squadrons, the group included night fighters, torpedo bombers, and service elements, all operating under extreme logistical strain.

MAG-33 flew a mix of:

- Combat Air Patrol (CAP) and Close Air Support (CAS)

- Armed reconnaissance

- Anti-kamikaze defense

Operations were conducted initially from escort carriers and later from

Kadena Airfield. This writing is focused on the story of the three Fighter Squadrons and is not designed to account for all MAG-33 units, nor should their story go untold.

3. VMF-322 and THE F4U-1D CORSAIR

Marine Fighter Squadron 322 (VMF-322) flew the F4U Corsair, an aircraft optimized for speed, firepower, and ruggedness—but demanding precise handling during take-off and landing, especially on short or damaged runways.

Key operational realities are reflected in the narrative:

• Landing accidents were a leading cause of aircraft loss, even after air superiority was achieved.

• Corsairs returning from CAS missions often carried structural damage, oil leaks, and compromised control surfaces.

• Runways at Kadena were under constant repair, frequently cratered by artillery and degraded by rain.

• Floodlights, steel matting, and coral fill introduced additional hazards during night and low-visibility operations.

These conditions made the act of returning often as dangerous as combat itself.

PHOTO CREDITS

Note: When available they are representative of the actual units, conditions, or events. When not, they highlight similar units, conditions, and events.

Bundesarchiv
Fig.6
Wikimedia Commons
Fig.2, 28, cover photo
NARA
Fig.16,31,37,41,42,44,45,48,50,53,55, 62
DOD
Fig.33
U.S. Navy
Fig.3,15,21,2,25,26,29,30,32,43,59
National WW II Museum
Fig.40
Australian War Memorial
Fig.38
Library of Congress
Fig.7,8,9,10 (Arnold T. Palmer)
World War Photos
Fig.11,12,13,20,39,47,49,52,54,57,58,60
US Marine Corps
Fig.5,14(Stan Abele),34,35,36,46,56,61,
U.S. Army
Fig.27

DEDICATION

For the men who flew low;
when the ground offered nowhere left for a man to go.

For those who did not come back; after stepping forward to answer the call.

Figure 62. Paying respects.

ACKNOWLEDGEMENTS

I would like to thank my family for their love, support and understanding while I was on this journey. Additional thanks go to the following individuals and organizations that answered my research queries!

Jared Calloway, Archivist
National Naval Aviation Museum

John Hodges, Archivist
Naval History and Heritage Command (NHHC)

Caitlin Hucik, Archivist
National Archives and Records Administration

Shawn P. Callahan, Ph. D., Director
US Marine Corp History Division

Melanie Austin (Editor Extraordinaire)
Seattle Editing